CW00458166

The Chicken Master

Chicken Akademy

Table of Contents

Recipes

ROASTED CHICKEN WITH ROSEMARY

ingredients

- 1/2 cup butter, cubed
- 4 tablespoons minced fresh rosemary or 2 tablespoons dried rosemary, crushed
- 2 tablespoons minced fresh parsley
- 1 teaspoon salt
- 1/2 teaspoon pepper
- 3 garlic cloves, minced
- 1 whole roasting chicken (5 to 6 pounds)
- 6 small red potatoes, halved
- 6 medium carrots, halved lengthwise and cut into 2-inch pieces
- 2 medium onions, quartered

directions

1. In a small saucepan, melt the butter; add seasonings and garlic.
2. Place chicken breast side up on wire rack in shallow roasting pan; Tie the drumsticks with kitchen twine.
3. Pour half of the butter mixture over the chicken. Arrange the potatoes, carrots, and onions around the chicken.
4. Drizzle the remaining butter mixture over the vegetables.
5. Bake at 350 ° for 1-1 / 2 hours. Enough of juices for cooking; bake for an additional 30-60 minutes, basting occasionally, until a thermometer inserted into the thickest part of the thigh reads 170 ° -175 °. (Cover loosely with foil if chicken is browning too quickly.)
6. Let stand 10-15 minutes, covered with aluminum foil if necessary, before cutting. Serve with vegetables.

PRESSURE-COOKER CHICKEN AND BACON WHITE CHILI

ingredients

- 1/2 pound bacon strips, coarsely chopped
- 6 boneless skinless chicken thighs
- 1 package (20 ounces) frozen corn
- 2 cans (15 ounces each) cannellini beans, rinsed and drained
- 2 cans (15 ounces each) black beans, rinsed and drained
- 2 cans (10 ounces each) diced tomatoes and green chiles
- 1 can (4 ounces) chopped green chiles
- 1 cup reduced-sodium chicken broth
- 1 tablespoon chili powder
- 1 teaspoon ground cumin
- 1 teaspoon onion powder
- 1 teaspoon minced garlic
- 1 envelope (1 ounce) ranch salad dressing mix
- 12 ounces cream cheese
- 2 cups shredded cheddar cheese
- Optional: Cubed avocado and sliced jalapeno

directions

1. Select the sauté or browning setting in a 6-quart container. electric pressure cooker; adjust to medium heat. Cook bacon until crisp, 5-6 minutes; remove the bacon and reserve. Brown chicken in bacon fat in batches until lightly browned, 5 to 6 minutes. Return bacon to skillet; top with corn and the next 11 ingredients in the order listed.
2. Locking cap; close the pressure release valve. Set pressure cook to high for 15 minutes. Let the pressure release naturally for 10 minutes; Quickly release any remaining pressure. Add the grated cheese until melted. If desired, serve with avocado and jalapeño.

SOUTHERN FRIED CHICKEN STRIPS

ingredients

- 1 large egg
- 1/2 cup buttermilk
- 1 cup all-purpose flour
- 1-1/2 teaspoons garlic powder
- 1-1/2 teaspoons pepper
- 1/2 teaspoon salt
- 1/2 teaspoon paprika
- 2 pounds chicken tenderloins
- Oil for deep-fat frying
- 2 tablespoons grated Parmesan cheese

directions

1. In a shallow bowl, beat the egg and buttermilk. In another shallow bowl, combine the flour, garlic powder, pepper, salt, and paprika. Dip the chicken in the egg mixture and then in the flour mixture.

2. In an electric skillet, heat the oil to 375 °. Fry the chicken, a few pieces at a time, for 2-3 minutes on each side or until no longer pink. Drain on paper towels. Sprinkle with cheese.

INSTANT POT SESAME CHICKEN

ingredients

- 1-1/2 pounds boneless skinless chicken breasts, cut into 1-inch pieces
- 1 tablespoon sesame oil
- 1/4 cup honey
- 1/4 cup soy sauce or gluten-free tamari soy sauce
- 1/4 cup water
- 3 garlic cloves, minced
- 1/4 teaspoon crushed red pepper flakes
- 3 teaspoons cornstarch
- 2 tablespoons cold water
- 1 tablespoon sesame seeds
- Hot cooked rice
- Thinly sliced green onions, optional

directions

1. Select the sauté or browning setting in a 6-quart container. Electric pressure cooker. Set to medium heat; add sesame oil. When oil is hot, brown chicken in batches. Press cancel. Return everything to the pressure cooker. In small bowl, whisk together honey, soy sauce, water, garlic, and pepper flakes; Stir in a pressure cooker. Locking cap; close the pressure release valve. Set to pressure cook on high for 4 minutes.
2. Quick release pressure. In small bowl, mix cornstarch and water until smooth; Stir in a pressure cooker. Select the stir fry setting and set to low heat. Cook over low heat, stirring constantly, until thickened, 1-2 minutes. Serve with rice. Sprinkle with sesame seeds and, if desired, green onions.

CREAMY CHICKEN ENCHILADAS

ingredients

- 1 package (8 ounces) cream cheese, softened
- 2 tablespoons water
- 2 teaspoons onion powder
- 2 teaspoons ground cumin
- 1/2 teaspoon salt
- 1/4 teaspoon pepper
- 5 cups diced cooked chicken
- 20 flour tortillas (6 inches), room temperature
- 2 cans (10-1/2 ounces each) condensed cream of chicken soup, undiluted
- 2 cups sour cream
- 1 cup 2% milk
- 2 cans (4 ounces each) chopped green chiles
- 2 cups shredded cheddar cheese

directions

1. **Preheat** the oven to 350 °. In a large bowl, beat the cream cheese, water, onion powder, cumin, salt, and pepper until smooth. Add the chicken.
2. Place 1/4 cup of the chicken mixture in the center of each tortilla. Roll up and position seam side down in two. baking dishes. In large bowl, combine soup, sour cream, milk, and chiles; Pour over the enchiladas.
3. Bake, uncovered, 30 to 40 minutes or until heated through. Sprinkle with cheese; bake 5 more minutes or until cheese is melted.

GRILLED HULI HULI CHICKEN

ingredients

- 1 cup packed brown sugar
- 3/4 cup ketchup
- 3/4 cup reduced-sodium soy sauce
- 1/3 cup sherry or chicken broth
- 2-1/2 teaspoons minced fresh gingerroot
- 1-1/2 teaspoons minced garlic
- 24 boneless skinless chicken thighs (about 6 pounds)

directions

1. In a small bowl, mix the first 6 ingredients. Reserve 1-1 / 3 cups for drizzling; cover and refrigerate. Divide remaining marinade between 2 large, shallow plates. Add 12 chicken thighs to each; turn to paste. Refrigerate, covered, for 8 hours or overnight.
2. Drain the chicken, discarding the marinade.
3. Grill chicken, covered, on a greased wire rack over medium heat for 6-8 minutes on each side or until thermometer reads 170 °; Enough occasionally with the reserved marinade for the last 5 minutes.

PUFF PASTRY CHICKEN POTPIE

ingredients

- 1 package (17.3 ounces) frozen puff pastry, thawed
- 2 pounds boneless skinless chicken breasts, cut into 1-inch pieces
- 1 teaspoon salt, divided
- 1 teaspoon pepper, divided
- 4 tablespoons butter, divided
- 1 large onion, chopped
- 2 garlic cloves, minced
- 1 teaspoon minced fresh thyme or 1/4 teaspoon dried thyme
- 1 teaspoon minced fresh sage or 1/4 teaspoon rubbed sage
- 1/2 cup all-purpose flour
- 1-1/2 cups chicken broth
- 1 cup plus 1 tablespoon half-and-half cream, divided
- 2 cups frozen mixed vegetables (about 10 ounces)
- 1 tablespoon lemon juice
- 1 large egg yolk

directions

1. Preheat the oven to 400 °. On a lightly floured surface, roll each puff pastry sheet into a 12x10-inch shape. rectangle. Cut 1 sheet crosswise into six 2-inch sheets. strips; cut the remaining sheet lengthwise into five 2-inch sheets. strips. On a baking sheet, weave the strips closely together to make a size of 12x10 inches. lattice. Freeze while you make the filling.
2. Mix the chicken with 1/2 teaspoon of salt and pepper. In a large skillet, heat 1 tablespoon of butter over medium-high heat; Sauté chicken until golden brown, 5 to 7 minutes. Remove from the pan.
3. In same skillet, heat remaining butter over medium-high heat; Sauté onion until tender, 5 to 7 minutes. Add garlic and herbs; cook 1 minute. Add flour until mixed; cook and stir 1 minute. Gradually add the broth and 1 cup of the cream. Boil stirring constantly; cook and stir until thickened, about 2 minutes.
4. Add vegetables, lemon juice, chicken, and remaining salt and pepper; boil again. Transfer to a greased 2-1 / 2-quart cup. elongated baking dish. Cover with lattice, trimming to fit.
5. Beat the egg yolk and the remaining cream; brush over the dough. Bake, uncovered, until bubbly and golden, 45 to 55 minutes. Cover loosely with aluminum foil if it starts to get too dark. Let stand 15 minutes before serving.

GRANDMA'S CHICKEN 'N' DUMPLING SOUP

ingredients

- 1 broiler/fryer chicken (3-1/2 to 4 pounds), cut up
- 2-1/4 quarts cold water
- 5 chicken bouillon cubes
- 6 whole peppercorns
- 3 whole cloves
- 1 can (10-3/4 ounces) condensed cream of chicken soup, undiluted
- 1 can (10-3/4 ounces) condensed cream of mushroom soup, undiluted
- 1-1/2 cups chopped carrots
- 1 cup fresh or frozen peas
- 1 cup chopped celery
- 1 cup chopped peeled potatoes
- 1/4 cup chopped onion
- 1-1/2 teaspoons seasoned salt
- 1/4 teaspoon pepper
- 1 bay leaf
- DUMPLINGS:
- 2 cups all-purpose flour
- 4 teaspoons baking powder
- 1 teaspoon salt
- 1/4 teaspoon pepper
- 1 large egg, beaten
- 2 tablespoons butter, melted
- 3/4 to 1 cup 2% milk
- Snipped fresh parsley, optional

directions

1. Place the chicken, water, broth, peppercorns, and cloves in a saucepan. Cover and bring to boil; skim foam. Reduce the heat; cover and simmer 45-60 minutes or until chicken is tender. Strain the broth; go back to the pot.

2. Remove chicken and set aside until cool enough to handle. Remove meat from bones; discard bones and skin and cut chicken into chunks. Cool the broth and remove the fat.

3. Return chicken to pot with soups, vegetables, and seasonings; bring to a boil. Reduce the heat; cover and simmer for 1 hour. To find out; increase heat to simmer. Discard the bay leaf.

4. For meatballs, combine dry ingredients in medium bowl. Add the egg, butter, and just enough milk to make a stiff, moist dough. Put teaspoons in the soup. Cover and cook without lifting the lid for 18-20 minutes. Sprinkle with parsley if desired.

SIMPLE CHICKEN ENCHILADAS

ingredients

- 1 can (10 ounces) enchilada sauce, divided
- 4 ounces cream cheese, cubed
- 1-1/2 cups salsa
- 2 cups cubed cooked chicken
- 1 can (15 ounces) pinto beans, rinsed and drained
- 1 can (4 ounces) chopped green chiles
- 10 flour tortillas (6 inches)
- 1 cup shredded Mexican cheese blend
- Optional: Shredded lettuce, chopped tomato, sour cream and sliced ripe olives

directions

1. Spoon 1/2 cup enchilada sauce into greased 13x9-inch plate. Baking dish. In a large saucepan, cook and stir cream cheese and sauce over medium heat until combined, 2-3 minutes. Add the chicken, beans, and chili peppers.
2. Place about 1/3 cup of the chicken mixture in the center of each tortilla. Roll up and place the seam side down over the sauce. Top with remaining enchilada sauce; sprinkle with cheese.
3. Cover and bake at 350 ° until heated through, 25-30 minutes. If desired, serve with lettuce, tomato, sour cream, and olives.

BEST-EVER FRIED CHICKEN

ingredients

- 1-3/4 cups all-purpose flour
- 1 tablespoon dried thyme
- 1 tablespoon paprika
- 2 teaspoons salt
- 2 teaspoons garlic powder
- 1 teaspoon pepper
- 1 large egg
- 1/3 cup whole milk
- 2 tablespoons lemon juice
- 1 broiler/fryer chicken (3 to 4 pounds), cut up
- Oil for deep-fat frying

directions

1. In a shallow bowl, mix the first 6 ingredients. In another shallow bowl, beat the egg, milk, and lemon juice until combined. Dip chicken in flour mixture to coat all sides; shake off excess. Dip in the egg mixture, then again in the flour mixture.
2. In an electric skillet or deep fryer, heat the oil to 375 °. Fry the chicken, a few pieces at a time, 6 to 10 minutes on each side or until golden brown and the chicken juices run clear. Drain on paper towels.

CONTEST-WINNING BROCCOLI CHICKEN CASSEROLE

ingredients

- 1 package (6 ounces) chicken stuffing mix
- 2 cups cubed cooked chicken
- 1 cup frozen broccoli florets, thawed
- 1 can (10-3/4 ounces) condensed broccoli cheese soup, undiluted
- 1 cup shredded cheddar cheese

directions

1. Preheat the oven to 350 °. Prepare stuffing mix according to package directions, using only 1-1 / 2 cups of water.
2. In a large bowl, combine chicken, broccoli, and soup; transfer to a greased 11x7 inch. Baking dish. Cover with filling; sprinkle with cheese. Bake, covered, 20 minutes. To find out; bake until heated through, 10-15 more minutes.
3. Freeze Option: Transfer individual servings from cooled casserole to freezer containers; freeze. To use, partially thaw in the refrigerator overnight. Transfer to a microwave safe plate and microwave, covered, on high until a thermometer inserted in the center reads 165 °, stirring occasionally and adding a little broth if necessary.

HERBED SLOW-COOKER CHICKEN

ingredients

- 1 tablespoon olive oil
- 1 teaspoon paprika
- 1/2 teaspoon garlic powder
- 1/2 teaspoon seasoned salt
- 1/2 teaspoon dried thyme
- 1/2 teaspoon dried basil
- 1/2 teaspoon pepper
- 1/2 teaspoon browning sauce, optional
- 4 bone-in chicken breast halves (8 ounces each)
- 1/2 cup chicken broth

directions

1. In a small bowl, combine the first 7 ingredients and, if desired, the browning sauce; rub over chicken. Place in a 5-quart container. Slow cooking pot; add the broth. Cover and simmer until chicken is tender, 4-5 hours.

CHICKEN & EGG NOODLE CASSEROLE

ingredients

- 6 cups uncooked egg noodles (about 12 ounces)
- 2 cans (10-3/4 ounces each) condensed cream of chicken soup, undiluted
- 1 cup sour cream
- 3/4 cup 2% milk
- 1/4 teaspoon salt
- 1/4 teaspoon pepper
- 3 cups cubed cooked chicken breasts
- 1 cup crushed Ritz crackers (about 20 crackers)
- 1/4 cup butter, melted

directions

1. Precalienta el horno a 350 °. Cocine los fideos de acuerdo con las instrucciones del paquete para al dente; drenar.
2. En un tazón grande, bata la sopa, la crema agria, la leche, la sal y la pimienta hasta que se combinen. Agrega el pollo y los fideos. Transfiera a una taza engrasada de 13x9 pulgadas. Plato de hornear. En un tazón pequeño, combine las galletas trituradas y la mantequilla; espolvorear por encima. Hornee hasta que esté burbujeante, de 30 a 35 minutos.

CHICKEN BARLEY SOUP

ingredients

- 1 broiler/fryer chicken (2 to 3 pounds), cut up
- 8 cups water
- 1-1/2 cups chopped carrots
- 1 cup chopped celery
- 1/2 cup medium pearl barley
- 1/2 cup chopped onion
- 1 teaspoon chicken bouillon granules
- 1 teaspoon salt, optional
- 1 bay leaf
- 1/2 teaspoon poultry seasoning
- 1/2 teaspoon pepper
- 1/2 teaspoon rubbed sage

directions

1. In a large pot, cook chicken in water until tender. Cool the broth and remove the fat. Set chicken aside until cool enough to handle. Remove meat from bones; discard the bones and cut the meat into cubes. Return the meat to the skillet along with the remaining ingredients. Bring to a boil. Reduce the fire; cover and simmer 1 hour or until vegetables and barley are tender. Discard the bay leaf.

CHICKEN ENCHILADA BAKE

ingredients

- 4-1/2 cups shredded rotisserie chicken
- 1 can (28 ounces) green enchilada sauce
- 1-1/4 cups sour cream
- 9 corn tortillas (6 inches), cut into 1-1/2-inch pieces
- 4 cups shredded Monterey Jack cheese
- Fresh minced parsley, optional

directions

1. Preheat the oven to 375 °. On a greased 13x9 in. baking sheet, place half of each of the following ingredients: chicken, enchilada sauce, sour cream, tortillas, and cheese. Repeat the layers.

2. Bake, covered, 40 minutes. To find out; bake until bubbly, about 10 more minutes. Let stand 15 minutes before serving. If desired, sprinkle with parsley.

3. Freeze Option: Cover and freeze casserole without baking. To use, partially thaw in the refrigerator overnight. Remove from refrigerator 30 minutes before baking. Preheat the oven to 375 °. Bake casserole as directed, increasing time as needed to fully heat and a thermometer inserted in center reads 165 °. Sprinkle with parsley. If desired, sprinkle with parsley.

QUICK CHICKEN PICCATA

ingredients

- 1/4 cup all-purpose flour
- 1/2 teaspoon salt
- 1/2 teaspoon pepper
- 4 boneless skinless chicken breast halves (4 ounces each)
- 1/4 cup butter, cubed
- 1/4 cup white wine or chicken broth
- 1 tablespoon lemon juice
- Minced fresh parsley, optional

directions

1. In a shallow bowl, mix together the flour, salt, and pepper. Pound the chicken breasts with a 1/2-inch meat mallet. thickness. Dip chicken in flour mixture to coat both sides; shake off excess.

2. In a large skillet, heat the butter over medium heat. Brown the chicken on both sides. Add wine; bring to a boil. Reduce the heat; simmer, uncovered, until chicken is no longer pink, 12 to 15 minutes. Drizzle with lemon juice. If desired, sprinkle with parsley.

CHICKEN WILD RICE SOUP

ingredients

- 2 quarts chicken broth
- 1/2 pound fresh mushrooms, chopped
- 1 cup finely chopped celery
- 1 cup shredded carrots
- 1/2 cup finely chopped onion
- 1 teaspoon chicken bouillon granules
- 1 teaspoon dried parsley flakes
- 1/4 teaspoon garlic powder
- 1/4 teaspoon dried thyme
- 1/4 cup butter, cubed
- 1/4 cup all-purpose flour
- 1 can (10-3/4 ounces) condensed cream of mushroom soup, undiluted
- 1/2 cup dry white wine or additional chicken broth
- 3 cups cooked wild rice
- 2 cups cubed cooked chicken

directions

1. In a large saucepan, combine the first 9 ingredients. Bring to a boil. Reduce the heat; cover and simmer for 30 minutes.
2. In a saucepan, melt the butter; add flour until smooth. Add the broth mixture little by little. Bring to a boil; cook and stir 2 minutes or until thickened. Whisk together the soup and wine. Add the rice and chicken; heat through.

CHICKEN POTPIE CASSEROLE

ingredients

- 1/3 cup butter, cubed
- 1-1/2 cups sliced fresh mush-rooms
- 2 medium carrots, sliced
- 1/2 medium onion, chopped
- 1/4 cup all-purpose flour
- 1 cup chicken broth
- 1 cup 2% milk
- 4 cups cubed cooked chicken
- 1 cup frozen peas
- 1 jar (2 ounces) diced pimien-tos, drained
- 1/2 teaspoon salt
- BISCUIT TOPPING:
- 2 cups all-purpose flour
- 4 teaspoons baking powder
- 2 teaspoons sugar
- 1/2 teaspoon salt
- 1/2 teaspoon cream of tartar
- 1/2 cup cold butter, cubed
- 2/3 cup 2% milk

directions

1. Preheat the oven to 400 °. In a large saucepan, heat the butter over medium heat. Add mush-rooms, carrots, and onion; cook and stir until tender.
2. Add flour until mixed; gradually add the broth and milk. Boil stirring constantly; cook and stir 2 minutes or until thickened. Add chicken, peas, bell peppers, and salt; heat through. Transfer to a greased 11x7-inch mug. Baking dish.
3. To coat, in a large bowl, whisk together the flour, baking powder, sugar, salt, and cream of tartar. Cut in butter until the mixture resembles coarse crumbs. Add the milk; Stir until moistened.
4. Turn on a lightly floured surface; knead gently 8 to 10 times. Stroke or roll dough to 1/2 inch. thickness; cut with a 2-1 / 2-in floured. cookie cutter. Place over chicken mixture. Bake, un-covered, 15 to 20 minutes or until cookies are golden brown.

PRESSURE-COOKER BUFFALO CHICKEN DIP

ingredients

- 1 pound boneless skinless chicken breasts
- 1 cup Buffalo wing sauce
- 2 tablespoons unsalted butter
- 2 packages (8 ounces each) cream cheese, softened, cubed
- 1/2 cup ranch salad dressing
- 1/2 cup sour cream
- 2 cups shredded cheddar cheese, divided
- 5 tablespoons crumbled blue cheese
- 1 green onion, sliced
- Tortilla chips

directions

1. Place the first 3 ingredients in a 6-quart container. Electric pressure cooker. Locking cap; close the pressure release valve. Set to pressure cook on high for 8 minutes. Quick release pressure. A thermometer inserted into the chicken should read at least 165 °.
2. Remove the chicken; mash with 2 forks. Return to the pressure cooker. Add the cream cheese, salad dressing, sour cream, and 1 cup of the cheddar cheese. Sprinkle the top with the remaining cheddar cheese, blue cheese, and green onions. Serve with tortilla chips.

BREADED RANCH CHICKEN

ingredients

- 1/4 cup unsalted butter, melted
- 3/4 cup crushed cornflakes
- 3/4 cup grated Parmesan cheese
- 1 envelope ranch salad dressing mix
- 8 boneless skinless chicken breast halves (4 ounces each)

directions

1. Place the butter in a shallow bowl. In another shallow bowl, combine the cornflakes, cheese, and salad dressing mix. Dip the chicken in butter, then roll in the corn flake mixture to coat.
2. Place in greased 13x9 in. Container. Baking dish. Bake, uncovered, at 350 ° until a thermometer reads 165 °, about 45 minutes.

CHICKEN BURRITOS

ingredients

- 6 tablespoons butter
- 1 large onion, chopped
- 1/4 cup chopped green pepper
- 1/2 cup all-purpose flour
- 3 cups chicken broth
- 1 can (10 ounces) diced tomatoes and green chiles, undrained
- 1 teaspoon ground cumin
- 1 teaspoon chili powder
- 1/2 teaspoon garlic powder
- 1/2 teaspoon salt
- 2 tablespoons chopped jalapeno pepper, optional
- 1 can (15 ounces) chili with beans
- 1 package (8 ounces) cream cheese, cubed
- 8 cups cubed cooked chicken
- 24 flour tortillas (6 inches), warmed
- 6 cups shredded Colby-Monterey Jack cheese
- Salsa, optional

directions

1. Preheat the oven to 350 °. In a Dutch oven, heat the butter over medium-high heat. Add the onion and bell pepper; cook and stir until tender. Add flour until mixed; gradually add the broth. Bring to a boil; cook and stir for 2 minutes. Reduce the heat; Add tomatoes, seasonings, and if desired, jalapeño. Cook 5 minutes. Add the chili and cream cheese; Stir until cream cheese melts. Add the chicken.
2. Place about 1/2 cup filling in center of each tortilla; sprinkle each with 1/4 cup Colby-Monterey Jack cheese. Fold bottom and sides over filling and roll. Place on 2 greased 13x9 in. Lids. baking dishes.
3. Bake, covered, 35 to 40 minutes or until heated through. If desired, serve with sauce.
4. Freeze option: fresh no-bake burritos; cover and freeze. To use, partially thaw in the refrigerator overnight. Remove from refrigerator 30 minutes before baking. Preheat the oven to 350 °. Cover burritos with foil; bake according to directions, increasing bake time to 50-55 minutes or until heated through and a thermometer inserted in the center reads 160 °.

CHICKEN TORTILLA BAKE

ingredients

- 3 cups shredded cooked chicken
- 2 cans (4 ounces each) chopped green chiles
- 1 cup chicken broth
- 1 can (10-3/4 ounces) condensed cream of mushroom soup, undiluted
- 1 can (10-3/4 ounces) condensed cream of chicken soup, undiluted
- 1 small onion, finely chopped
- 12 corn tortillas, warmed
- 2 cups shredded cheddar cheese
- Sour cream and green onions, optional

directions

1. In a large bowl, combine chicken, chiles, broth, soups, and onion; set aside. Place half of the tortillas in a greased 13x9-inch layer. baking dish, cut to fit pan if desired. Top with half the chicken mixture and half the cheese. Repeat the layers.

2. Bake, uncovered, at 350 ° for 30 minutes or until heated through.

3. Freeze Option: Cover and freeze casserole without baking. To use, partially thaw in the refrigerator overnight. Remove from refrigerator 30 minutes before baking. Preheat the oven to 350 °. Bake casserole as directed, increasing time as needed to heat up and a thermometer inserted in the center reads 165 °. If desired, serve with sour cream and green onions.

CREAMY CHICKEN VOL-AU-VENT

ingredients

- 1 package (17.30 ounces) frozen puff pastry, thawed
- 1 large egg
- 1 tablespoon water
- 6 bacon strips
- 2 medium leeks (white portion only), sliced
- 1 medium sweet yellow pepper, diced
- 1 cup shredded rotisserie chicken
- 8 ounces cream cheese, softened
- 1/4 teaspoon salt
- 1/4 teaspoon pepper
- Minced fresh parsley plus additional ground pepper

directions

1. Preheat the oven to 400 °. On a lightly floured surface, unfold 1 puff pastry sheet. Using a 3-1 / 4-in. round cutter, cut six circles. Place on a parchment lined baking sheet.
2. Unfold the remaining puff pastry sheet. Cut 6 more circles with the 3-1 / 4-in. round cutter with a 2-1 / 2-in. cutter, cut out the center of the circles. Place the rings on top of the circles on the baking sheet. Place the center circles on the baking sheet as well. In a small bowl, beat the egg and water; brush the cakes. Let cool 15 minutes. Bake until dark golden brown, 20-25 minutes. Let cool on a rack.
3. Meanwhile, in a large skillet, cook bacon over medium heat until crisp. Remove to paper towels to drain. Discard all but 1 tablespoon drippings. Add leeks and pepper to fat; cook and stir over medium-high heat until tender, 5-7 minutes. Reduce heat to low; Add the bacon, chicken, cream cheese, salt, and pepper. Cook and stir until blended; Remove from heat.
4. When cool enough to handle, hollow out the cakes with a small knife. Fill with the chicken mixture. Sprinkle with parsley and pepper. Serve with small cakes in the center on the side.

CONTEST-WINNING CHICKEN WITH MUSHROOM SAUCE

ingredients

- 2 teaspoons cornstarch
- 1/2 cup fat-free milk
- 4 boneless skinless chicken breast halves (4 ounces each)
- 1 tablespoon olive oil
- 1 tablespoon butter
- 1/2 pound sliced fresh mushrooms
- 1/2 medium onion, thinly sliced
- 1/4 cup sherry or chicken broth
- 1/2 teaspoon salt
- 1/8 teaspoon pepper

directions

1. Mix the cornstarch and milk until smooth. Pound chicken with a 1/4-inch meat mallet. thickness.
2. In large nonstick skillet, heat oil over medium heat; cook chicken until no longer pink, 5-6 minutes per side. Remove from the pan.
3. In the same skillet, heat the butter over medium-high heat; sauté the mushrooms and onion until tender. Add the sherry, salt, and pepper; bring to a boil. Stir the cornstarch mixture and add to the skillet. Bring to a boil again; cook and stir until thickened, 1-2 minutes. Return chicken to skillet; heat through.

CHICKEN AND RICE CASSEROLE

ingredients

- 4 cups cooked white rice or a combination of wild and white rice
- 4 cups diced cooked chicken
- 1/2 cup slivered almonds
- 1 small onion, chopped
- 1 can (8 ounces) sliced water chestnuts, drained
- 1 package (10 ounces) frozen peas, thawed
- 3/4 cup chopped celery
- 1 can (10-3/4 ounces) condensed cream of celery soup, undiluted
- 1 can (10-3/4 ounces) condensed cream of chicken soup, undiluted
- 1 cup mayonnaise
- 2 teaspoons lemon juice
- 1 teaspoon salt
- 2 cups crushed potato chips
- Paprika

directions

1. Preheat the oven to 350 °. On a greased 13x9 in. baking dish, combine first 7 ingredients. In a large bowl, combine the soups, mayonnaise, lemon juice, and salt. Pour over the chicken mixture and toss to coat.
2. Sprinkle with French fries and paprika. Bake until heated through, about 1 hour.

PRESSURE-COOKER CHICKEN TORTILLA SOUP

ingredients

- 1 tablespoon canola oil
- 1 medium onion, chopped
- 3 garlic cloves, minced
- 1 pound boneless skinless chicken breasts
- 1 carton (32 ounces) reduced-sodium chicken broth
- 1 can (15 ounces) black beans, rinsed and drained
- 1 can (14 ounces) fire-roasted diced tomatoes
- 1-1/2 cups frozen corn
- 1 tablespoon chili powder
- 1 tablespoon ground cumin
- 1 teaspoon paprika
- 1/2 teaspoon salt
- 1/4 teaspoon pepper
- 1/4 cup minced fresh cilantro
- Optional: Crumbled tortilla chips, chopped avocado, jalapeno peppers and lime wedges

directions

1. Select the stir fry setting on a 6-qt. electric pressure cooker and set to high temperature; add the oil. Add the onion; cook and stir 6 to 8 minutes or until tender. Add the garlic; cook 1 minute more. Add the next 10 ingredients. Stir. Locking cap; close the pressure release valve.

2. Set to pressure cook on high for 8 minutes. Let the pressure release naturally for 12 minutes, then quickly release any remaining pressure.

3. Remove chicken from pressure cooker. Mash with 2 forks; return to pressure cooker. Add the cilantro and stir. If desired, serve with garnishes.

CREAMY CHICKEN RICE SOUP

ingredients

- 1 tablespoon canola oil
- 1 medium carrot, chopped
- 1 celery rib, chopped
- 1/2 cup chopped onion
- 1/2 teaspoon minced garlic
- 1/3 cup uncooked long grain rice
- 3/4 teaspoon dried basil
- 1/4 teaspoon pepper
- 2 cans (14-1/2 ounces each) reduced-sodium chicken broth
- 3 tablespoons all-purpose flour
- 1 can (5 ounces) evaporated milk
- 2 cups cubed cooked chicken breast

directions

1. In a large saucepan, heat the oil over medium-high heat; Sauté carrot, celery and onion until tender. Add the garlic; cook and stir 1 minute. Add rice, seasonings, and broth; bring to a boil. Reduce the heat; simmer, covered, until rice is tender, about 15 minutes.
2. Mix the flour and milk until smooth; Stir into soup. Bring to a boil; cook and stir until thickened, about 2 minutes. Add the chicken; heat through.

CHICKEN PICCATA WITH LEMON SAUCE

ingredients

- 8 boneless skinless chicken breast halves (4 ounces each)
- 1/2 cup egg substitute
- 2 tablespoons plus 1/4 cup dry white wine or chicken broth, divided
- 5 tablespoons lemon juice, divided
- 3 garlic cloves, minced
- 1/8 teaspoon hot pepper sauce
- 1/2 cup all-purpose flour
- 1/2 cup grated Parmesan cheese
- 1/4 cup minced fresh parsley
- 1/2 teaspoon salt
- 3 teaspoons olive oil, divided
- 2 tablespoons butter

directions

1. Flatten chicken to 1/4 inch. thickness. In a shallow dish, combine the egg substitute, 2 tablespoons of wine, 2 tablespoons of lemon juice, garlic, and hot pepper sauce. In another shallow dish, combine the flour, Parmesan cheese, parsley, and salt. Coat the chicken with the flour mixture, dip it in the egg substitute mixture, and then coat it again with the flour mixture.
2. In a large nonstick skillet, brown 4 chicken breast halves in 1-1 / 2 teaspoons oil for 3-5 minutes on each side or until juices run clear. Remove and keep warm. Drain the drips. Repeat with the rest of the chicken and the oil. Remove and keep warm.
3. In the same skillet, melt the butter. Add the remaining wine and lemon juice. Bring to a boil. Boil, uncovered, until the sauce is reduced by a quarter. Drizzle over chicken.

HONEY CHICKEN STIR-FRY

ingredients

- 2 teaspoons cornstarch
- 1 tablespoon cold water
- 3 teaspoons olive oil, divided
- 1 pound boneless skinless chicken breasts, cut into 1-inch pieces
- 1 garlic clove, minced
- 3 tablespoons honey
- 2 tablespoons reduced-sodium soy sauce
- 1/8 teaspoon salt
- 1/8 teaspoon pepper
- 1 package (16 ounces) frozen broccoli stir-fry vegetable blend
- Hot cooked rice, optional

directions

1. Mix cornstarch and water until smooth. In large nonstick skillet, heat 2 teaspoons oil over medium-high heat; sauté chicken and garlic 1 minute. Add honey, I am sauce, salt and pepper; cook and stir until chicken is no longer pink, 2-3 minutes. Remove from the pan.

2. In the same skillet, sauté the vegetable mixture in the remaining oil until tender, 4-5 minutes. Return the chicken to the skillet. Stir cornstarch mixture and add to skillet; bring to a boil. Cook and stir until thickened, about 1 minute. Serve with rice if desired.

DUTCH OVEN ENCHILADAS

ingredients

- 3 cups shredded cooked chicken
- 1 can (15 ounces) black beans, rinsed and drained
- 1 can (10-1/2 ounces) condensed cream of chicken soup, undiluted
- 1 can (10 ounces) green enchilada sauce
- 1 can (4 ounces) chopped green chiles
- 1/4 cup minced fresh cilantro
- 1 tablespoon lime juice
- 9 corn tortillas (6 inches)
- 3 cups shredded Colby-Monterey Jack cheese
- Optional: Minced fresh cilantro, salsa, sour cream and lime wedges

directions

1. Preheat the oven to 350 °. In a large bowl, combine the first 7 ingredients. Spread 1/4 cup of the chicken mixture over the bottom of the pot. Top with 3 tortillas, overlapping and breaking to fit, one-third of the chicken mixture and one-third of the cheese. Repeat twice.
2. Bake, covered, until thermometer reads 165 °, 50-60 minutes. If desired, serve with additional cilantro, salsa, sour cream, and lemon wedges.

CONTEST-WINNING PEANUT CHICKEN STIR-FRY

ingredients

- × 8 ounces uncooked thick rice noodles
- × 1/3 cup water
- × 1/4 cup reduced-sodium soy sauce
- × 1/4 cup peanut butter
- × 4-1/2 teaspoons brown sugar
- × 1 tablespoon lemon juice
- × 2 garlic cloves, minced
- × 1/2 teaspoon crushed red pepper flakes
- × 2 tablespoons canola oil, divided
- × 1 pound boneless skinless chicken breasts, cut into 1/2-inch strips
- × 1 bunch broccoli, cut into florets
- × 1/2 cup shredded carrot
- × Sesame seeds, optional

directions

1. Cook noodles according to package directions. Meanwhile, in small bowl, combine water, soy sauce, peanut butter, brown sugar, lemon juice, garlic, and pepper flakes; set aside.

2. In a large skillet, heat 1 tablespoon of the oil over medium-high heat. Add the chicken; sauté until no longer pink, 3-4 minutes. Remove from the pan.

3. Sauté the broccoli and carrot in the remaining oil until crisp-tender, 4 to 6 minutes. Add soy sauce mixture; bring to a boil. Cook and stir until sauce thickens, 1-2 minutes. Return chicken to skillet; heat through. Drain the noodles; Mix with the chicken mixture in a skillet. If desired, sprinkle with sesame seeds.

TROPICAL CHICKEN CAULIFLOWER RICE BOWLS

ingredients

- 1 fresh pineapple, peeled, cored and cubed (about 3 cups), divided
- 1/2 cup plain or coconut Greek yogurt
- 2 tablespoons plus 1/2 cup chopped fresh cilantro, divided
- 3 tablespoons lime juice, divided
- 3/4 teaspoon salt, divided
- 1/4 teaspoon crushed red pepper flakes
- 1/8 teaspoon chili powder
- 4 boneless skinless chicken breast halves (6 ounces each)
- 3 cups fresh cauliflower florets (about 1/2 small cauliflower)
- 1 tablespoon canola oil
- 1 small red onion, finely chopped
- Optional: Toasted sweetened shredded coconut or lime wedges

directions

1. For the marinade, place 1 cup pineapple, yogurt, 2 tablespoons coriander and lime juice, 1/4 teaspoon salt, pepper flakes, and chili powder in a food processor; process until blended. In a large bowl, mix chicken with marinade; refrigerate, covered, 1-3 hours.
2. In a clean food processor, pulse cauliflower until it resembles rice (do not over-process). In large skillet, heat oil over medium-high heat; Sauté onion until lightly browned, 3 to 5 minutes. Add the cauliflower; cook and stir until lightly browned, 5-7 minutes. Add 1 cup pineapple and the remaining lemon juice and salt; cook, covered, over medium heat until cauliflower is tender, 3-5 minutes. Add the remaining cilantro. Stay warm.
3. Preheat the grill or broiler. Drain the chicken, discarding the marinade. Place chicken on greased grill over medium heat or greased 15x10x1-inch aluminum foil. bread. Grill, covered, or broil 4 inches from heat until thermometer reads 165 °, 4-6 minutes per side. Let stand 5 minutes before cutting.
4. To serve, divide cauliflower mixture into 4 bowls. Top with chicken, remaining pineapple and, if desired, coconut and lime slices.

WHITE BEAN CHICKEN CHILI

ingredients

- 3/4 pound boneless skinless chicken breasts, cut into 1-1/4-inch pieces
- 1/4 teaspoon salt
- 1/4 teaspoon pepper
- 2 tablespoons olive oil, divided
- 1 medium onion, chopped
- 1 jalapeno pepper, seeded and chopped
- 4 garlic cloves, minced
- 2 teaspoons dried oregano
- 1 teaspoon ground cumin
- 2 cans (15 ounces each) cannellini beans, rinsed and drained, divided
- 2-1/2 cups chicken broth, divided
- 1-1/2 cups shredded cheddar cheese
- Optional toppings: sliced avocado, quartered cherry tomatoes and chopped cilantro

directions

1. Mix the chicken with salt and pepper. In a large skillet, heat 1 tablespoon oil over medium-high heat; sauté the chicken until golden brown. Transfer to 3 quarts. Slow cooking pot.
2. In the same skillet, heat the remaining oil over medium heat; sauté onion until tender. Add jalapeño, garlic, oregano, and cumin; cook and stir 2 minutes. Add to slow cooker.
3. In a bowl, mash 1 cup of beans; add 1/2 cup of broth. Add bean mixture and remaining whole beans and broth to chicken mixture.
4. Cook, covered, over low heat until chicken is tender, 3-3-1 / 2 hours. Stir before serving. Sprinkle with cheese; add toppings if desired.
5. Freeze Option: Freeze chilled chili in freezer containers. To use, partially thaw in the refrigerator overnight. Heat in a saucepan, stirring occasionally and adding a little broth or water if necessary.

BLACK BEAN CHICKEN WITH RICE

ingredients

- 3 teaspoons chili powder
- 1 teaspoon ground cumin
- 1 teaspoon pepper
- 1/4 teaspoon salt
- 4 boneless skinless chicken breast halves (4 ounces each)
- 2 teaspoons canola oil
- 1 can (15 ounces) black beans, rinsed and drained
- 1 cup frozen corn
- 1 cup salsa
- 2 cups hot cooked brown rice

directions

1. In a small bowl, mix seasonings; sprinkle over both sides of the chicken. In a large nonstick skillet, heat the oil over medium heat. Brown the chicken on both sides.
2. Add beans, corn, and salsa to skillet; cook, covered, 10-15 minutes or until a thermometer inserted into the chicken reads 165 °. Remove chicken from skillet; cut in slices. Serve with the bean and rice mixture.

AIR FRYER CHICKEN TENDERS

ingredients

- 1/2 cup panko bread crumbs
- 1/2 cup potato sticks, crushed
- 1/2 cup crushed cheese crackers
- 1/4 cup grated Parmesan cheese
- 2 bacon strips, cooked and crumbled
- 2 teaspoons minced fresh chives
- 1/4 cup butter, melted
- 1 tablespoon sour cream
- 1 pound chicken tenderloins
- Additional sour cream and chives

directions

1. Preheat the fryer to 400 °. In a shallow bowl, combine the first 6 ingredients. In another shallow bowl, whiskey butter and sour cream. Dip chicken in butter mixture, then crumb mixture, patting to help coating adhere.

2. In batches, place chicken in single layer on greased pan in deep fryer basket; spray with cooking spray. Cook until the layer is golden brown and the chicken is no longer pink, 7 to 8 minutes on each side. Serve with additional sour cream and chives.

CHICKEN NOODLE CASSEROLE

ingredients

- 1 can (10-3/4 ounces) condensed cream of chicken soup, undiluted
- 1/2 cup mayonnaise
- 2 tablespoons lemon juice
- 2 cups cubed cooked chicken
- 1 small onion, chopped
- 1/4 cup chopped green pepper
- 1/4 cup chopped sweet red pepper
- 1 cup shredded Monterey Jack cheese, divided
- 1 cup shredded sharp cheddar cheese, divided
- 12 ounces egg noodles, cooked and drained

directions

1. In a large bowl, combine the soup, mayonnaise, and lemon juice. Add the chicken, onion, bell peppers, 1/2 cup Monterey Jack cheese, and 1/2 cup cheddar cheese. Add the noodles and stir to coat.
2. Transfer to a greased 2-quart cup. Baking dish. Bake, uncovered, at 350 ° for 30-35 minutes. Sprinkle with the remaining cheeses. Bake until cheese is melted, about 10 more minutes.
3. Freeze Option: Sprinkle remaining cheeses over no-bake casserole. Cover and freeze. To use, partially thaw in the refrigerator overnight. Remove from refrigerator 30 minutes before baking. Preheat the oven to 350 °. Bake casserole as directed, increasing time as needed to heat up and a thermometer inserted in the center reads 165 °.

LEMON CHICKEN WITH ORZO

ingredients

- 1/3 cup all-purpose flour
- 1 teaspoon garlic powder
- 1 pound boneless skinless chicken breasts
- 3/4 teaspoon salt, divided
- 1/2 teaspoon pepper
- 2 tablespoons olive oil
- 1 can (14-1/2 ounces) reduced-sodium chicken broth
- 1-1/4 cups uncooked whole wheat orzo pasta
- 2 cups chopped fresh spinach
- 1 cup grape tomatoes, halved
- 3 tablespoons lemon juice
- 2 tablespoons minced fresh basil
- Lemon wedges, optional

directions

1. In a shallow bowl, mix together the flour and garlic powder. Cut the chicken into 1-1 / 2 in. pieces; pound each with a 1/4 in. meat mallet. thickness. Sprinkle with 1/2 teaspoon of salt and pepper. Dip both sides of chicken in flour mixture to coat lightly; shake off excess.
2. In a large skillet, heat the oil over medium heat. Add the chicken; cook 3 to 4 minutes on each side or until golden brown and chicken is no longer pink. Remove from skillet; keeping warm. Clean the pan.
3. In the same skillet, bring the broth to a boil; Stir in orzo. Bring to a boil again. Reduce the heat; simmer, covered, 8 to 10 minutes or until tender. Add spinach, tomatoes, lemon juice, basil, and remaining salt; Remove from heat. Return the chicken to the skillet. If desired, serve with lemon wedges.

TERIYAKI CHICKEN THIGHS

ingredients

- 3 pounds boneless skinless chicken thighs
- 3/4 cup sugar
- 3/4 cup reduced-sodium soy sauce
- 1/3 cup cider vinegar
- 1 garlic clove, minced
- 3/4 teaspoon ground ginger
- 1/4 teaspoon pepper
- 4 teaspoons cornstarch
- 4 teaspoons cold water
- Hot cooked rice, optional

directions

1. Place chicken in 4-5 quart container. Slow cooking pot. In a small bowl, combine the sugar, soy sauce, vinegar, garlic, ginger, and pepper; pour over chicken. Cook, covered, over low heat for 4-5 hours or until chicken is tender.
2. Place chicken in serving platter; keeping warm. Transfer cooking juices to small saucepan; skim fat. Bring the cooking juices to a boil. In a small bowl, mix cornstarch and cold water until smooth; Stir in the cooking juices. Bring to a boil again; cook and stir 1-2 minutes or until thickened. Serve with chicken and, if desired, rice.

CREAMY CHICKEN AND PASTA

ingredients

- 2 cups uncooked penne pasta
- 2 cups sliced fresh mushrooms
- 1 cup sliced green onions
- 2 tablespoons butter
- 1/2 cup white wine or chicken broth
- 1 teaspoon minced garlic
- 1 tablespoon all-purpose flour
- 1/3 cup water
- 1 cup heavy whipping cream
- 2 cups cubed cooked chicken
- 2 tablespoons capers, drained
- 1/4 teaspoon salt
- 1/8 teaspoon pepper
- Shredded Parmesan cheese

directions

1. Cook pasta according to package directions. Meanwhile, in a large skillet, sauté mushrooms and onions in butter for 4-5 minutes or until tender. Add wine or broth and garlic. Bring to a boil; cook until liquid is reduced by half, about 5 minutes.
2. Combine flour and water until smooth; gradually add to mushroom mixture. Bring to a boil. Reduce the heat; cook and stir 2 minutes or until thickened. Add the cream. Bring to a boil. Reduce the heat; simmer, uncovered, 4-5 minutes or until heated through.
3. Drain the pasta. Add the pasta, chicken, capers, salt, and pepper to the cream sauce. Cook for 3-4 minutes or until heated through. Sprinkle with Parmesan cheese.

COMFORTING CHICKEN NOODLE SOUP

ingredients

- 2 quarts water
- 8 teaspoons chicken bouillon granules
- 6-1/2 cups uncooked wide egg noodles
- 2 cans (10-3/4 ounces each) condensed cream of chicken soup, undiluted
- 3 cups cubed cooked chicken
- 1 cup sour cream
- Minced fresh parsley

directions

1. In a large saucepan, bring the water and broth to a boil. Add the noodles; cook, uncovered, until tender, about 10 minutes. Do not drain. Add the soup and chicken; heat through.
2. Remove from the fire; Add sour cream. Sprinkle with chopped parsley.

CHICKEN TATER BAKE

ingredients

- 2 cans (10-3/4 ounces each) condensed cream of chicken soup, undiluted
- 1/2 cup 2% milk
- 1/4 cup butter, cubed
- 3 cups cubed cooked chicken
- 1 package (16 ounces) frozen peas and carrots, thawed
- 1-1/2 cups shredded cheddar cheese, divided
- 1 package (32 ounces) frozen Tater Tots

directions

1. In a large saucepan, combine the soup, milk, and butter. Cook and stir over medium heat until completely hot. Remove from the fire; Add the chicken, peas and carrots, and 1 cup of the cheese.
2. Transfer to 2 greased 8 in. Faucets. square baking dishes. Top with Tater Tots.
3. Cover and freeze 1 saucepan for up to 3 months. Bake the remaining casserole at 400 ° until bubbly, 25-30 minutes. Sprinkle with 1/4 cup cheese; bake until cheese is melted, about 5 more minutes.
4. To use a frozen casserole: Remove from the freezer 30 minutes before baking (do not defrost). Sprinkle with 1/4 cup of cheese. Cover and bake at 350 ° until heated through, 1-1 / 2 to 1-3 / 4 hours.

SAVORY RUBBED ROAST CHICKEN

ingredients

- 2 teaspoons paprika
- 1 teaspoon salt
- 1 teaspoon onion powder
- 1 teaspoon white pepper
- 1 teaspoon cayenne pepper
- 1 teaspoon dried thyme
- 3/4 teaspoon garlic powder
- 1/2 teaspoon pepper
- 1 roasting chicken (6 to 7 pounds)
- 1 large onion, cut into wedges

directions

1. Preheat the oven to 350 °. In a small bowl, mix the first eight ingredients.
2. Pat the chicken dry and place on a wire rack in a roasting pan, breast side up. Rub the seasoning mixture over the outside and inside of the chicken. Place the onion inside the cavity. Tuck wings under chicken; tie the drumsticks together.
3. Broil for 2 to 2-1 / 2 hours or until a thermometer inserted in the thickest part of the thigh reads 170 ° -175 °. (Cover lightly with foil if chicken is browning too quickly.) Remove chicken from oven; tent with foil. Let stand 15 minutes before cutting.

CAJUN CHICKEN & PASTA

ingredients

- 1 pound boneless skinless chicken breasts, cut into 2x1/2-in. strips
- 3 teaspoons Cajun seasoning
- 8 ounces uncooked penne pasta (about 2-1/3 cups)
- 2 tablespoons butter, divided
- 1 small sweet red pepper, diced
- 1 small green pepper, diced
- 1/2 cup sliced fresh mushrooms
- 4 green onions, chopped
- 1 cup heavy whipping cream
- 1/2 teaspoon salt
- 1/4 teaspoon dried basil
- 1/4 teaspoon lemon-pepper seasoning
- 1/4 teaspoon garlic powder
- Pepper to taste
- Chopped plum tomatoes
- Minced fresh basil
- Shredded Parmesan cheese

directions

1. Toss chicken with Cajun seasoning; let it rest for 15 minutes. Cook pasta according to package directions; to drain.
2. In a large skillet, heat 1 tablespoon of butter over medium-high heat; sauté chicken until no longer pink, 5-6 minutes. Remove from the pan.
3. In same skillet, heat remaining butter over medium-high heat; Sauté peppers, mushrooms, and green onions until peppers are crisp-tender, 6 to 8 minutes. Add cream and seasonings; bring to a boil. Cook and stir until slightly thickened, 4-6 minutes. Add pasta and chicken; heat through. Top with tomatoes and basil. Sprinkle with cheese.

BEST EVER FRIED CHICKEN WINGS

ingredients

- 4 pounds chicken wings
- 2 teaspoons kosher salt
- Oil for deep-fat frying
- BUFFALO WING SAUCE:
- 3/4 cup Louisiana-style hot sauce
- 1/4 cup unsalted butter, cubed
- 2 tablespoons molasses
- 1/4 teaspoon cayenne pepper
- SPICY THAI SAUCE:
- 1 tablespoon canola oil
- 1 teaspoon grated fresh gingerroot
- 1 garlic clove, minced
- 1 minced Thai chile pepper or 1/4 teaspoon crushed red pepper flakes
- 1/4 cup packed dark brown sugar
- 2 tablespoons lime juice
- 2 tablespoons minced fresh cilantro
- 1 tablespoon fish sauce
- SPICY BARBECUE SAUCE:
- 3/4 cup barbecue sauce
- 2 chipotle peppers in adobo sauce, finely chopped
- 2 tablespoons honey
- 1 tablespoon cider vinegar
- Thinly sliced green onions, optional

directions

1. With a sharp knife, cut the 2 wing joints; discard the wingtips. Pat the chicken dry with paper towels. Toss the wings with kosher salt. Place on a wire rack in a 15x10x1 in. Space. baking sheet. Refrigerate at least 1 hour or overnight.

2. In an electric skillet or deep fryer, heat the oil to 375 °. Fry wings in batches until skin is crisp and meat is tender, 8 to 10 minutes. Drain on paper towels.

3. For the chicken wing sauce, bring the hot sauce to a boil in a small saucepan. Remove from heat; Mix butter 1 piece at a time. Add the molasses and cayenne pepper.

4. For the Thai sauce, heat the oil in a small saucepan over medium heat. Add the ginger, garlic, and chili; cook and stir until fragrant, about 2 minutes. Add the brown sugar and lime juice. Bring to a boil; cook until slightly thickened, about 5 minutes. Add the cilantro and fish sauce.

5. For the barbecue sauce, heat the prepared barbecue sauce in a small saucepan over medium heat. Add the chipotle peppers, honey, and vinegar. Bring to a boil; cook and stir until slightly thickened, about 5 minutes.

6. Toss the wings with 1 of the willows. If desired, sprinkle with green onion slices.

CHICKEN CASSEROLE

ingredients

- 1/2 cup chopped celery
- 1/4 cup chopped onion
- 2 tablespoons chopped green pepper
- 2 tablespoons butter
- 2 cups cubed cooked chicken
- 1 jar (4-1/2 ounces) sliced mushrooms, drained
- 6 pimiento-stuffed olives, sliced
- 1 can (10-3/4 ounces) condensed cream of chicken soup, undiluted
- 1 cup milk
- 5 cups cooked wide egg noodles
- TOPPING:
- 1/2 cup cornflake crumbs
- 1/4 cup shredded cheddar cheese
- 2 tablespoons butter, melted

directions

1. In a large skillet, sauté the celery, onion, and green pepper in butter. Remove from the fire; Add the chicken, mushrooms, olives, soup, milk, and noodles.
2. Transfer to 2 quarts. Baking dish. Cover and bake at 325 ° for 25 minutes. Meanwhile, combine topping ingredients. Sprinkle around edge of casserole; bake 5 more minutes or until cheese is melted.

CHICKEN WITH PINEAPPLE

ingredients

- 4 boneless skinless chicken breast halves (4 ounces each)
- 1 tablespoon all-purpose flour
- 1 tablespoon canola oil
- 2 cans (8 ounces each) unsweetened pineapple chunks
- 1 teaspoon cornstarch
- 1 tablespoon honey
- 1 tablespoon reduced-sodium teriyaki sauce or reduced-sodium soy sauce
- 1/8 teaspoon pepper
- Hot cooked rice

directions

1. Flatten the chicken to 1/4 inch. thickness. Place the flour in a large, shallow dish; add chicken and turn to coat.
2. In a large skillet, brown chicken over medium heat in oil until juices run clear, 3 to 5 minutes on each side. Remove and keep warm. Drain the pineapple, reserving 1/4 cup of the juice. (Discard the remaining juice or save it for another use.)
3. In a small bowl, combine cornstarch and reserved juice until smooth. Gradually add to the pan. Add the honey, teriyaki sauce, and pepper. Bring to a boil. Cook and stir until thickened, about 30 seconds. Add pineapple and chicken; heat through. Serve with rice.

LEMON CHICKEN PASTA

ingredients

- 4 boneless skinless chicken breast halves (6 ounces each)
- 1 teaspoon salt, divided
- 1/4 teaspoon plus 1/8 teaspoon pepper, divided
- 1/2 cup all-purpose flour
- 8 ounces uncooked capellini or angel hair pasta
- 3 tablespoons olive oil, divided
- 1/4 cup peeled and thinly sliced garlic cloves (about 12 cloves)
- 1 cup white wine or chicken broth
- 2 tablespoons lemon juice
- 1/2 cup grated Parmigiano-Reggiano cheese
- 1/3 cup plus 3 tablespoons minced fresh parsley, divided
- Lemon wedges, optional

directions

1. Pound chicken breasts with a 1/4-inch meat mallet. thickness. Sprinkle with 1/2 teaspoon of salt and 1/4 teaspoon of pepper. Place the flour in a shallow bowl. Dip chicken in flour to coat both sides; shake off excess.

2. Cook pasta according to package directions for al dente. Meanwhile, in a large skillet, heat 2 tablespoons of oil over medium heat. Add the chicken; cook 2-3 minutes on each side or until no longer pink. Remove and keep warm.

3. In the same skillet, heat the remaining oil over medium heat; add the garlic. Cook and stir 30 to 60 seconds or until garlic is lightly browned. Add wine to skillet; increase heat to medium-high. Cook, stirring to loosen the browned bits from the pan, until the liquid is reduced by half. Stir in the lemon juice.

4. Drain pasta, reserving 1/2 cup water for pasta; place in a large bowl. Add the cheese, 1/3 cup of the parsley, half of the garlic mixture, and the rest of the salt and pepper; Stir to combine, adding enough reserved pasta water to moisten the pasta. Serve with chicken. Drizzle with remaining garlic mixture; sprinkle with the remaining parsley. If desired, serve with lemon wedges.

ASIAN CHICKEN THIGHS

ingredients

- 5 teaspoons olive oil
- 5 bone-in chicken thighs (about 1-3/4 pounds), skin removed
- 1/3 cup water
- 1/4 cup packed brown sugar
- 2 tablespoons orange juice
- 2 tablespoons reduced-sodium soy sauce
- 2 tablespoons ketchup
- 1 tablespoon white vinegar
- 4 garlic cloves, minced
- 1/2 teaspoon crushed red pepper flakes
- 1/4 teaspoon Chinese five-spice powder
- 2 teaspoons cornstarch
- 2 tablespoons cold water
- Sliced green onions
- Hot cooked rice, optional

directions

1. In a large skillet, heat the oil over medium heat. Add the chicken; cook until golden brown, 8 to 10 minutes on each side. In a small bowl, whiskey water, brown sugar, orange juice, soy sauce, tomato sauce, vinegar, garlic, pepper flakes, and five-spice powder. Pour over the chicken. Bring to a boil. Reduce the heat; simmer, uncovered, until chicken is tender, 30 to 35 minutes, turning occasionally.
2. In a small bowl, mix cornstarch and cold water until smooth; Stir in the skillet. Bring to a boil; cook and stir until sauce thickens, about 1 minute. Sprinkle with green onions. If desired, serve with rice.
3. Freezing option: chilled chicken. Freeze in freezer containers. To use, partially thaw in the refrigerator overnight. Heat slowly in a covered skillet until a thermometer inserted into the chicken reads 165 °, stirring occasionally and adding a little water if necessary.

CHICKEN AND FALAFEL WAFFLES

ingredients

- 3/4 cup plain Greek yogurt
- 3/4 cup chopped peeled cucumber
- 1 cup chopped green onions, divided
- 2 tablespoons minced fresh mint plus additional for garnish
- 1/4 teaspoon salt
- 1/8 teaspoon pepper
- 1 can (15 ounces) no-salt-added garbanzo beans or chickpeas, rinsed and drained
- 1 large egg, room temperature
- 1/3 cup fresh parsley leaves
- 4-1/2 teaspoons gluten-free all-purpose baking flour
- 2 tablespoons Moroccan seasoning (ras el hanout), divided
- 1-1/2 cups shredded cooked chicken
- 1-1/2 cups reduced-sugar apricot preserves
- 3/4 cup chili sauce

directions

1. Preheat the waffle iron. In a small bowl, combine the yogurt, cucumber, 1/2 cup green onions, 2 tablespoons mint, salt, and pepper.
2. Cover and refrigerate until serving.
3. Place the chickpeas, egg, parsley, gluten-free flour, 1 tablespoon of Moroccan seasoning, and remaining green onions in a blender.
4. Cover and pulse until combined (batter should be thick). Bake the waffles according to the manufacturer's instructions until golden brown.
5. Meanwhile, in small skillet, combine chicken, preserves, chili sauce, and remaining Moroccan seasoning; heat through. Serve with waffles. Top with the additional yogurt and mint mixture.

TOMATO-MELON CHICKEN SALAD

ingredients

- 4 medium tomatoes, cut into wedges
- 2 cups cubed seedless water-melon
- 1 cup fresh raspberries
- 1/4 cup minced fresh basil
- 1/4 cup olive oil
- 2 tablespoons balsamic vine-gar
- 1/4 teaspoon salt
- 1/4 teaspoon pepper
- 9 cups torn mixed salad greens
- 4 grilled chicken breasts (4 ounces each), sliced

directions

1. In a large bowl, combine the tomatoes, water-melon, and raspberries.
2. In a small bowl, whisk together the basil, oil, vin-egar, salt, and pepper.
3. Drizzle over tomato mixture; stir to coat.
4. Divide salad leaves among 6 serving plates; top with tomato mixture and chicken.

EASY WHITE CHICKEN CHILI

ingredients

- 1 pound lean ground chicken
- 1 medium onion, chopped
- 2 cans (15 ounces each) cannellini beans, rinsed and drained
- 1 can (4 ounces) chopped green chiles
- 1 teaspoon ground cumin
- 1/2 teaspoon dried oregano
- 1/4 teaspoon pepper
- 1 can (14-1/2 ounces) reduced-sodium chicken broth
- Optional toppings: Reduced-fat sour cream, shredded cheddar cheese and chopped fresh cilantro

directions

1. In a large saucepan, cook chicken and onion over medium-high heat until chicken is no longer pink, 6 to 8 minutes, breaking chicken into crumbs.
2. Pour 1 can of beans into small bowl; lightly mash. Add ground beans, remaining can of beans, chiles, seasonings, and broth to chicken mixture; bring to a boil. Reduce the heat; simmer, covered, until flavors are blended, 12 to 15 minutes. Serve with toppings of your choice.
3. Freeze Option: Freeze chilled chili in freezer containers. To use, partially thaw in the refrigerator overnight. Heat in saucepan, stirring occasionally; add broth if necessary.

GOAT CHEESE AND SPINACH STUFFED CHICKEN

ingredients

- 1-1/2 cups fresh spinach, chopped
- 1/3 cup julienned soft sun-dried tomatoes (not packed in oil), chopped
- 1/4 cup crumbled goat cheese
- 2 garlic cloves, minced
- 1/2 teaspoon pepper, divided
- 1/4 teaspoon salt, divided
- 2 boneless skinless chicken breasts (6 ounces each)
- 1 tablespoon olive oil, divided
- 1/2 pound fresh asparagus, trimmed
- Aged balsamic vinegar or balsamic glaze, optional

directions

1. Preheat the oven to 400 °. In a small bowl, combine the spinach, sun-dried tomatoes, goat cheese, garlic, 1/4 teaspoon pepper, and 1/8 teaspoon salt.

2. Cut a pocket horizontally in the thickest part of each chicken breast. Fill with spinach mixture; Secure with toothpicks.

3. In an 8 in. In a cast iron or oven skillet, heat 1-1 / 2 teaspoons oil over medium heat. Brown the chicken on each side. Place in the oven; bake 10 minutes.

4. Mix asparagus with remaining 1-1 / 2 teaspoon oil, 1/4 teaspoon pepper, and 1/8 teaspoon salt; add to skillet. Bake until a thermometer inserted into the chicken reads 165 ° and the asparagus is tender, 10-15 minutes longer. If desired, sprinkle with vinegar. Discard toothpicks before serving.

CHICKEN & DUMPLING CASSEROLE

ingredients

- 1/2 cup chopped onion
- 1/2 cup chopped celery
- 1/4 cup butter, cubed
- 2 garlic cloves, minced
- 1/2 cup all-purpose flour
- 2 teaspoons sugar
- 1 teaspoon salt
- 1 teaspoon dried basil
- 1/2 teaspoon pepper
- 4 cups chicken broth
- 1 package (10 ounces) frozen green peas
- 4 cups cubed cooked chicken
- DUMPLINGS:
- 2 cups biscuit/baking mix
- 2 teaspoons dried basil
- 2/3 cup 2% milk

directions

1. Preheat the oven to 350 °. In a large saucepan, sauté the onion and celery in butter until tender. Add the garlic; cook 1 minute more. Add the flour, sugar, salt, basil, and pepper until combined. Gradually add the broth; bring to a boil. Cook and stir 1 minute or until thickened; reduce heat. Add the peas and cook 5 minutes, stirring constantly. Add the chicken. Pour into a greased 13x9-inch container. Baking dish.

2. For the meatballs, in a small bowl, combine the baking mixture and basil. Add the milk with a fork until moistened. Pour mounding tablespoons over the chicken mixture.

3. Bake, uncovered, 30 minutes. Cover and bake 10 more minutes or until toothpick inserted into ball of dough comes out clean.

CURRIED CHICKEN SOUP

ingredients

- 4 teaspoons curry powder
- 1/2 teaspoon salt
- 1/2 teaspoon pepper
- 1/2 teaspoon cayenne pepper
- 1 pound boneless skinless chicken breasts, cut into 1-inch cubes
- 3 medium carrots, chopped
- 1 medium sweet red pepper, chopped
- 1 small onion, chopped
- 2 tablespoons olive oil
- 1 garlic clove, minced
- 1 can (15 ounces) garbanzo beans or chickpeas, rinsed and drained
- 1 can (14-1/2 ounces) chicken broth
- 1 can (14-1/2 ounces) diced tomatoes, drained
- 1 cup water
- 1 can (13.66 ounces) coconut milk
- 3/4 cup minced fresh cilantro

directions

1. In a large, shallow dish, combine the curry, salt, pepper, and cayenne pepper. Add the chicken, a few chunks at a time, and flip to coat.
2. In a large saucepan over medium heat, cook the chicken, carrots, red pepper, and onion in oil for 4 minutes.
3. Add the garlic; cook 1-2 minutes longer or until chicken is golden brown and vegetables are tender; to drain.
4. Add the chickpeas, broth, tomatoes, and water.
5. Bring to a boil. Reduce the heat; cover and simmer for 30 minutes. Stir in the coconut milk; heat through. Garnish the portions with cilantro.

SPICED GRILLED CHICKEN WITH CILANTRO LIME BUTTER

ingredients

- 1 tablespoon chili powder
- 1 tablespoon brown sugar
- 2 teaspoons ground cinnamon
- 1 teaspoon baking cocoa
- 1/2 teaspoon salt
- 1/2 teaspoon pepper
- 3 tablespoons olive oil
- 1 tablespoon balsamic vinegar
- 6 bone-in chicken breast halves (8 ounces each)
- CILANTRO LIME BUTTER:
- 1/3 cup butter, melted
- 1/4 cup minced fresh cilantro
- 2 tablespoons finely chopped red onion
- 1 tablespoon lime juice
- 1 serrano pepper, finely chopped
- 1/8 teaspoon pepper

directions

1. In a small bowl, combine the first eight ingredients. Brush over the chicken.
2. Place chicken skin side down on grill. Grill, covered, over medium indirect heat for 15 minutes.
3. Turn; Grill 20-25 more minutes or until thermometer reads 165 °.
4. Meanwhile, in a small bowl, combine the butter ingredients. Drizzle over chicken before serving.

GRILLED BASIL CHICKEN AND TOMATOES

ingredients

- 3/4 cup balsamic vinegar
- 1/4 cup tightly packed fresh basil leaves
- 2 tablespoons olive oil
- 1 garlic clove, minced
- 1/2 teaspoon salt
- 8 plum tomatoes
- 4 boneless skinless chicken breast halves (4 ounces each)

directions

1. For the marinade, place the first five ingredients in a blender.
2. Cut 4 tomatoes into quarters and add to blender; cover and process until combined. Cut the remaining tomatoes in half to grill.
3. In bowl, combine chicken and 2/3 cup marinade; refrigerate, covered, 1 hour, turning occasionally.
4. Reserve the remaining marinade for serving.
5. Drain the chicken, discarding the marinade. Place the chicken on a greased grill over medium heat.
6. Grill chicken covered until thermometer reads 165 °, 4 to 6 minutes per side.
7. Grill the covered tomatoes over medium heat until lightly golden, 2 to 4 minutes per side. Serve the chicken and tomatoes with the reserved marinade.

PAN-ROASTED CHICKEN AND VEGETABLES

ingredients

- 2 pounds red potatoes (about 6 medium), cut into 3/4-inch pieces
- 1 large onion, coarsely chopped
- 2 tablespoons olive oil
- 3 garlic cloves, minced
- 1-1/4 teaspoons salt, divided
- 1 teaspoon dried rosemary, crushed, divided
- 3/4 teaspoon pepper, divided
- 1/2 teaspoon paprika
- 6 bone-in chicken thighs (about 2-1/4 pounds), skin removed
- 6 cups fresh baby spinach (about 6 ounces)

directions

1. Preheat the oven to 425 °. In a large bowl, combine potatoes, onion, oil, garlic, 3/4 teaspoon salt, 1/2 teaspoon rosemary, and 1/2 teaspoon pepper; stir to coat. Transfer to 15x10x1 in. baking pan covered with cooking spray.
2. In a small bowl, combine the paprika and the remaining salt, rosemary, and pepper.
3. Sprinkle chicken with paprika mixture; place over vegetables. Grill until a thermometer inserted into the chicken reads 170 ° -175 ° and the vegetables are tender, 35-40 minutes.
4. Place chicken in serving platter; keeping warm. Top the vegetables with spinach.
5. Roast until vegetables are tender and spinach is wilted, another 8 to 10 minutes. Stir vegetables to combine; serve with chicken.

CARIBBEAN CHICKEN

ingredients

- 1/2 cup lemon juice
- 1/3 cup honey
- 3 tablespoons canola oil
- 6 green onions, sliced
- 3 jalapeno peppers, seeded and chopped
- 3 teaspoons dried thyme
- 3/4 teaspoon salt
- 1/4 teaspoon ground allspice
- 1/4 teaspoon ground nutmeg
- 6 boneless skinless chicken breast halves (4 ounces each)

directions

1. In a blender, combine the first 9 ingredients; cover and process until smooth. Pour 1/2 cup into small bowl for basting; cover and refrigerate.
2. Pour the remaining marinade into a shallow bowl or plate.
3. Add chicken and turn to coat; cover and refrigerate for up to 6 hours.
4. Drain the chicken, discarding the marinade. On a greased grill rack, cook chicken, covered, over medium heat or broil 4 inches from heat until a thermometer reads 165 °, 4-6 minutes on each side, basting frequently with reserved marinade.

CHICKEN THIGHS WITH SHALLOTS & SPINACH

ingredients

- 6 boneless skinless chicken thighs (about 1-1/2 pounds)
- 1/2 teaspoon seasoned salt
- 1/2 teaspoon pepper
- 1-1/2 teaspoons olive oil
- 4 shallots, thinly sliced
- 1/3 cup white wine or reduced-sodium chicken broth
- 1 package (10 ounces) fresh spinach, trimmed
- 1/4 teaspoon salt
- 1/4 cup reduced-fat sour cream

directions

1. Sprinkle the chicken with salt and pepper. In a large nonstick skillet, heat the oil over medium heat.
2. Add the chicken; cook until a thermometer reads 170 °, about 6 minutes on each side. Remove from skillet; keeping warm.
3. In the same skillet, cook and stir shallots until tender. Add wine; bring to a boil. Cook until the wine is reduced by half.
4. Add the spinach and salt; cook and stir until spinach is soft. Add sour cream; serve with chicken.
5. Freeze Option: Before adding the sour cream, chill the chicken and spinach mixture. Freeze in freezer containers.
6. To use, partially thaw in the refrigerator overnight. Heat slowly in covered skillet, stirring occasionally, until a thermometer inserted into the chicken reads 170 °. Add sour cream.

CHICKEN KORMA

ingredients

- 1 large potato, peeled and cut into 1/2-inch cubes
- 1 large onion, chopped
- 1 cinnamon stick (3 inches)
- 1 bay leaf
- 3 whole cloves
- 1 tablespoon canola oil
- 1 pound boneless skinless chicken breasts, cut into 1/2-inch cubes
- 1 garlic clove, minced
- 1 teaspoon curry powder
- 1/2 teaspoon minced fresh gingerroot
- 2 medium tomatoes, seeded and chopped
- 1 teaspoon salt
- 1/2 cup sour cream
- Hot cooked rice

directions

1. Place the potato in a small saucepan and cover with water. Bring to a boil. Reduce the heat; cover and cook until tender, 10 to 15 minutes. To drain.
2. In a large skillet, sauté the onion, cinnamon, bay leaf and cloves in oil until the onion is tender.
3. Add chicken, garlic, curry, and ginger; cook and stir 1 minute more. Add the tomatoes, salt, and potato.
4. Cover and cook until chicken is no longer pink, 10 to 15 minutes.
5. Remove from the fire; discard the cinnamon, bay leaf, and cloves. Add sour cream. Serve with rice.

CHICKEN WITH ROSEMARY BUTTER SAUCE

ingredients

- 4 boneless skinless chicken breast halves (6 ounces each)
- 4 tablespoons butter, divided
- 1/2 cup white wine or chicken broth
- 1/2 cup heavy whipping cream
- 1 tablespoon minced fresh rosemary

directions

1. In a large skillet over medium heat, cook chicken in 1 tablespoon of butter until thermometer reads 165 °, 4-5 minutes on each side. Remove and keep warm.
2. Add wine to skillet; cook over medium-low heat, stirring to loosen browned bits from skillet. Add the cream and bring to a boil.
3. Reduce the heat; cook and stir until slightly thickened. Add the rosemary and the remaining 3 tablespoons of butter until combined. Serve the sauce with the chicken.

BROILED CHICKEN & ARTICHOKES

ingredients

- 8 boneless skinless chicken thighs (about 2 pounds)
- 2 jars (7-1/2 ounces each) marinated quartered artichoke hearts, drained
- 2 tablespoons olive oil
- 1 teaspoon salt
- 1/2 teaspoon pepper
- 1/4 cup shredded Parmesan cheese
- 2 tablespoons minced fresh parsley

directions

1. Preheat the boiler. In a large bowl, toss the chicken and artichokes with oil, salt, and pepper.
2. Transfer to a roasting pan.
3. Grill 3 inches from heat for 8 to 10 minutes or until a thermometer inserted into the chicken reads 170 °, turning the chicken and artichokes halfway through.
4. Sprinkle with cheese.
5. Grill 1-2 more minutes or until cheese is melted. Sprinkle with parsley.

Anatomy of the Chicken

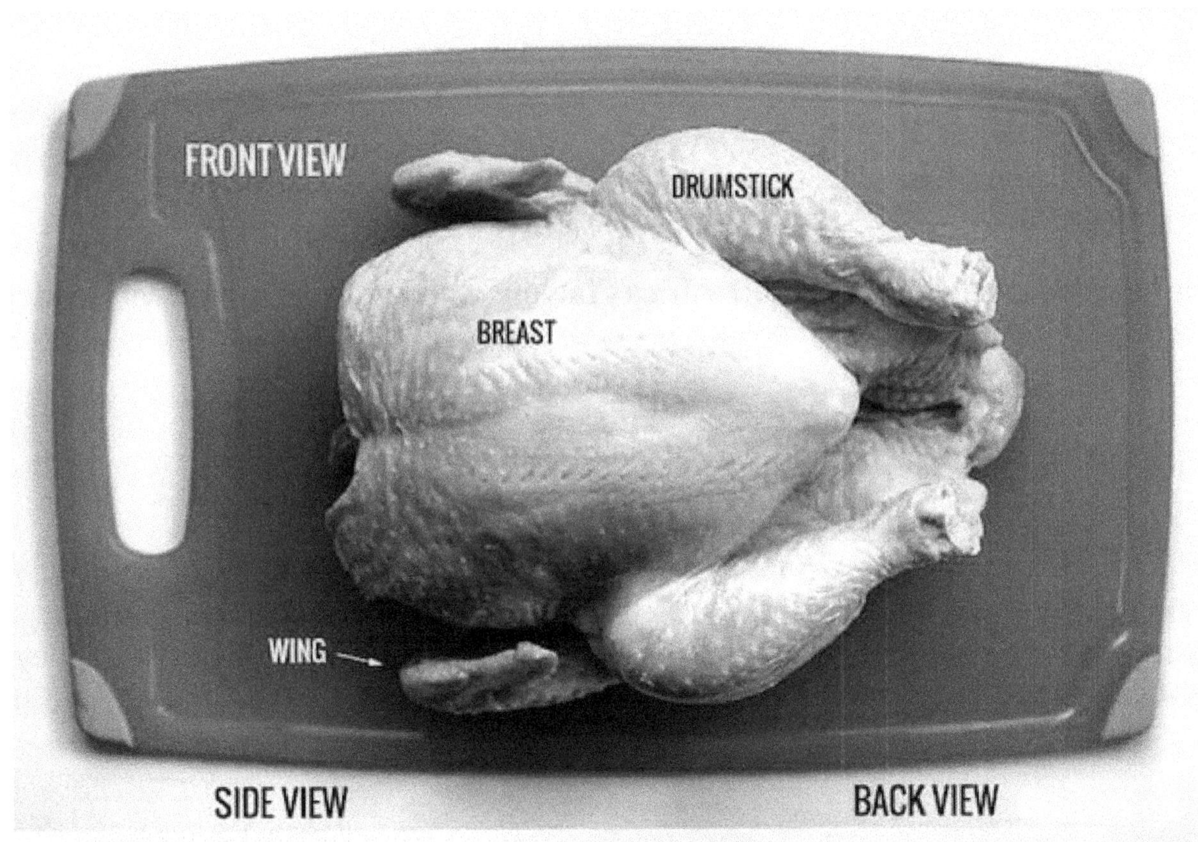
FRONT VIEW
DRUMSTICK
BREAST
WING
SIDE VIEW
BACK VIEW

THIGH
WING

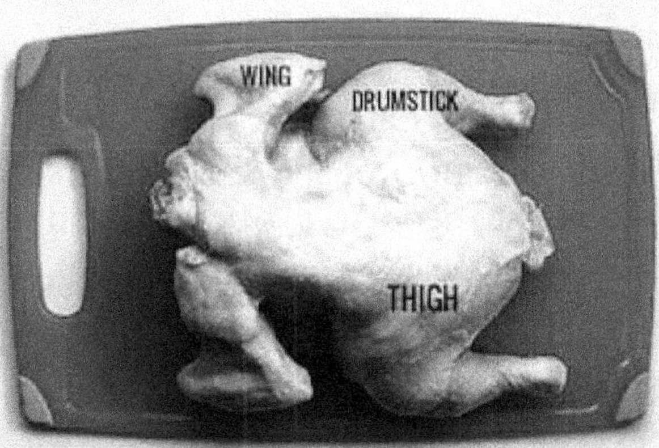
WING
DRUMSTICK
THIGH

ANATOMY OF THE CHICKEN

Head

The head is the talkie part of South Africa's famous walkie-talkies and stewing and braising are the best ways to cook it.

Breast

This very lean cut is best cooked quickly to keep them moist, for instance grilling, frying and braaiing. When stewing for braising breasts, don't overcook them as they will become dry and stringy.

Wing

Wings are high in fat and can withstand heat without becoming dry. They therefore are suited to deep- frying, braaiing and roasting. But however you cook them,

Tail

TAILS The tail is often attached to the thigh. It is packed with flavour because it contains a lot of fat and, thanks to the large skin area, becomes very crispy.

ANATOMY OF THE CHICKEN

Neck

This bony cut has very little meat but is an inexpensive way to flavour sauces and stock.

Thighs

Like drumsticks, thighs will be rather tough if not cooked properly. They have loads of fantastic flavour and are best when roasted or braised slowly or added to stews.

Drumstic

This popular cut could also be tough if it hasn't been cooked for long enough. The delicious dark brown meat particularly takes time and drumsticks taste best when they've been roasted, stewed, braised or braaied.

Feet

The other half of walkie-talkies, chicken feet are bony and low on meat. Once cooked, though, they are tender and can be eaten whole. Braai or grill them if you like crisp, crunchy skin.

HOW MANY CALORIES IN CHICKEN?

Chicken tenders

263 calories per 3.5 ounces (100 grams)

Back

137 calories per 3.5 ounces (100 grams)

Dark meat

125 calories per 3.5 ounces (100 grams)

Light meat

114 calories per 3.5 ounces (100 grams)

HOW MANY CALORIES IN CHICKEN?

Breast

A 3.5-ounce (100-gram) serving of chicken breast provides 165 calories, 31 grams of protein and 3.6 grams of fat.

Thigh

A 3.5-ounce (100-gram) serving of chicken thigh provides 209 calories, 26 grams of protein and 10.9 grams of fat.

Wing

Per 3.5 ounces (100 grams), chicken wings provide 203 calories, 30.5 grams of protein and 8.1 grams of fat.

Drumstick

Per 3.5 ounces (100 grams), chicken drumsticks have 172 calories, 28.3 grams of protein and 5.7 grams of fat.

Skin

While a skinless chicken breast is 284 calories with 80% protein and 20% fat, those numbers **dramatically** shift when you include the skin. One boneless, cooked chicken breast with skin (196 grams) contains: Calories: 386, Protein: 58.4 grams, Fat: 15.2 grams

COOKING METHODS

Grilling

This is one of the more common cooking methods, as it tends to require less added fat.

Baking or roasting

These other common methods are sufficient when you don't have access to a grill.

Broiling

This is similar to grilling, but you usually do it in a standard oven or toaster oven.

Braising

Lightly panfry the chicken and then cook it covered, submerged in liquid, for an extended time at a lower temperature.

COOKING METHODS

Fried

The chicken is submerged in hot cooking oil in either a pan or deep fryer. This creates a crisp outer coating but adds quite a bit of fat.

Baking or roasting

These other common methods are sufficient when you don't have access to a grill.

Boiling

You submerge the meat in boiling water and cook it until the internal temperature reaches 165°F (74°C). This is the leanest method, as it doesn't require added fats. Still, some may find the texture lacking.

Quick Recipes

Lemon Garlic Chicken

Place whole roasting chicken in baker with one whole lemon and one head of garlic (unpeeled) in cavity of chicken. Season with salt and pepper. Cover with lid and cook for 1-1/2 hours at 425°. (Try with an orange too.)

Roasted Turkey Breast

Place turkey breast in baker; place 6-8 small red skinned potatoes, halved, around turkey. Add 1/2 cup white wine and 2 cloves pressed garlic. Season with salt and pepper. Cover with lid. Bake at 350°F for 1-1/2 hours. Uncover for last 15-20 minutes. Let stand 5 minutes before slicing.

Honey Mustard Chicken

Place roasting chicken in the baker and pour fat free honey mustard dressing over the top. Cover with lid. Roast for 1-1/2 hours at 425°F.

3 CHEFS' TIPS
A little know-how can make life in the kitchen a lot easier

Done Yet

There are two ways to check if a chicken breast is done.
The first is to insert the tip of a small knife into the thickest part of the meat. If the juices run clear, it is cooked; if it's still pink,
you need to cook longer. Alternatively, make a small incision in the thickest part of the breast. If the meat is completely white and you don't see any pink meat, the brisket is done. The juices will also be clear. This method also works for testing whole chickens and other chicken pieces.

Slicing chicken breast for stir fry

Place the chicken breast, smooth-side down on a cutting board.
Cut it diagonally into 1 cm strips and halve each strip lengthwise into longer, thinner strips before cutting them diagonally across the fibres to keep it tender.

Butterflying chicken breasts for schnitzels

Place the chicken breast smooth side down on a cutting board. Make a shallow incision along one side and continue as if you were trying to cut the breast into two identical halves. Stop just before cutting it all the way so the top and bottom half open like a book. With a meat mallet, gently beat the thickest part until it is finer and more uniform. Butterfly breasts can also be stuffed with any filling you like.

TIPS AND TRICKS

Keeping it Clean

- Once the chicken is thawed, do not refreeze it.
- Do not allow raw chicken to come into contact with other foods, cooked or raw.
- Always wash your hands, utensils, and surfaces that have come in contact with raw chicken with hot, soapy water.
- Keep a separate cutting board for raw meat to avoid cross contamination.
- Always make sure the meat is well cooked to kill any harmful bacteria that may have been lurking.

When buying chicken

Always look for chicken that has an even colour with no blemishes or bruises. The meat should look moist and plump and have a neutral smell. Check that the packaging hasn't been damaged in any way. When buying frozen chicken, make sure that the meat is frozen solid and does not have any soft areas where it has begun to defrost – and do remember to check the sell-by-date too.

Storing Chicken

Always refrigerate or freeze chicken as soon as possible after purchasing it. If the package is damaged or soggy and you are going to cook it within two days, remove the chicken, pat dry with kitchen paper, and place on a plate. Cover with cling film or aluminum foil and place plate on bottom rack of refrigerator. That way you won't contaminate other food if it leaks. If you want to freeze the chicken at home, remove it from the package, pat dry, and seal it in an airtight bag.

TIPS AND TRICKS

Stop Breast Drying

How to stop the breast from drying out when MAKING roast chicken.
Roast the chicken breast-side down for two thirds of the cooking time. This way, all the juices will run down into the breast meat and keep it moist. Once you are ready to crisp the skin, carefully turn the chicken breast-side up and roast until golden.

How Tos and Hacks

Chicken salad. Place chicken breast side up on cutting board. Pull the
the leg and thigh away from the body and use your fingers to find the hip joint in the crease. Insert the tip of a large knife into the joint and cut through the skin, meat, and joint to separate the thigh and leg from the body. Repeat on the other side. Use the same method to separate the leg from the thigh and cut the wings from the body. To remove the chicken breast, cut the breast to divide the carcass in two. Cut off all the bone and cartilage in the breasts.
You will now have two of each: thighs, drumsticks, wings, and breasts. Add the carcass to soups, stews or casseroles for flavor and remove the bones just before serving.

How to defrost a whole chicken

Thawing a frozen chicken is best done overnight in the fridge. Place it in a large bowl or on a plate to prevent the juices from dripping in the fridge. Before cooking it, check inside the cavity to see that there is no more ice. If pressed for time, put the bird in a bucket of cold water in the sink, but be sure to keep the water cold to prevent bacteria from growing.

TIPS AND TRICKS

Getting a golden skin

Check that the skin is completely dry, rub the whole bird generously with oil and season well.
Uncover the chicken 20-30 minutes before the end of the cooking time and place it on a shallow baking tray or on an oven rack on a tray to allow the dry heat to come into contact with as much skin as possible. Roast until the skin is crisp and glassy

Chicken and food poisoning

Raw chicken may contain natural bacteria, which could be dangerous if it hasn't been stored properly. Salmonella and campylobacter, which are linked to food poisoning and gastro, are among the most common.

3 DIPS FOR CHICKEN NUGGETS

Garlic and lemon mayo

Stir 2 finely chopped garlic cloves and zest and juice of 1/2 lemon into 1 cup (250 ml) Mayonnaise.

Tomato relish

Finely chop 3 small sherkins and 3 pickeled onions and stir into 3/4 cup (180ml) tomato sauce.

Sweet and sour

Stir together 3/4 cup (180 ml) pineapple juice, 1/4 cup (60 ml) apple cider vinegar, 1/4 cup (60 ml) brown sugar, 2 tbsp (30 ml) tomato cauce and 1 tbps (15 ml) cornflour. Thicker over a low heat.

Quick Recipes

Chicken Pot Pie

Simmer a couple of boneless, skinless chicken breasts, cool and dice. Microwave diced potatoes, carrots, celery, onion, green beans, or peas. Combine with cornstarch thickened chicken broth (from simmered chicken), and pour into pie crust lined baker (you can use ready-made Pillsbury), then top with the other crust, crimp, brush with milk , sprinkle with herbs, sesame seeds or a little Parmesan and bake at 350 ° for about 40 min.

Cranberry Chicken

Mix one can of whole berry cranberries w/ can of cream of mushroom soup and one packet of onion soup mix. Pour over top of chicken in baker. Cover with lid, place in oven; bake for 1-1/2 hours at 425.

Chicken and Vegetables

Place chicken (skin on or off) in baker. Place chopped onion, celery and carrots around chicken. Sprinkle with 1/2 package of Good Seasons Italian Dressing mix. Place lid on top. Bake at 350° for 1 hour.

FRAN'S CHICKEN

ingredients

- 4 whole chicken breasts, skinned and boned
- 2 cans cream of mushroom soup
- 1 can milk
- 16 oz. sour cream
- 1 sm. bag Pepperidge Farm stuffing

directions

1. Prepare the filling according to the instructions on the package and let it cool.
2. Cook chicken, cut breasts in half and place in 9 x 13 "baking dish.
3. Mix soup

CREAMY HAM AND CHICKEN MEDLEY

ingredients

- 1 tbsp. butter
- 1/2 c. fresh mushrooms, sliced 1/3 c. butter
- 1/3 c. flour
- 2 1/2 - 3 c. milk, divided 1 c. Half & Half
- 1 c. parmesan cheese, freshly grated 1/2 tsp. salt
- 1/4 tsp. black pepper 1/4 tsp. nutmeg
- 2 c. chopped cooked chicken 2 c. chopped cooked ham
- 2 (10 oz.) pkgs. frozen puff pastry shells, baked

directions

1. Melt 1 tablespoon of butter in large saucepan over medium heat; add mushrooms and cook until tender, stirring constantly.
2. Remove from the saucepan and reserve.
3. Melt 1/3 cup butter in saucepan over low heat; add flour, stirring until smooth.
4. Cook 1 minute, stirring constantly.
5. Gradually add 2 1/2 cups of milk; cook over medium heat, stirring constantly, until thickened and bubbly.
6. Add the whipped cream and the next five ingredients.
7. Cook, stirring constantly, until cheese is melted and mixture is smooth; add the chicken and ham.
8. Add enough remaining 1/2 cup milk for a finer consistency.
9. To serve, pour in the shells. The yield of the sauce is 10 shells. Note: This can be made a day in advance and refrigerated.
10. Either in the microwave or place on the stove to warm gently. It can be served over pasta.
11. Serve with a crunchy green salad.

Anatomy of the Chicken

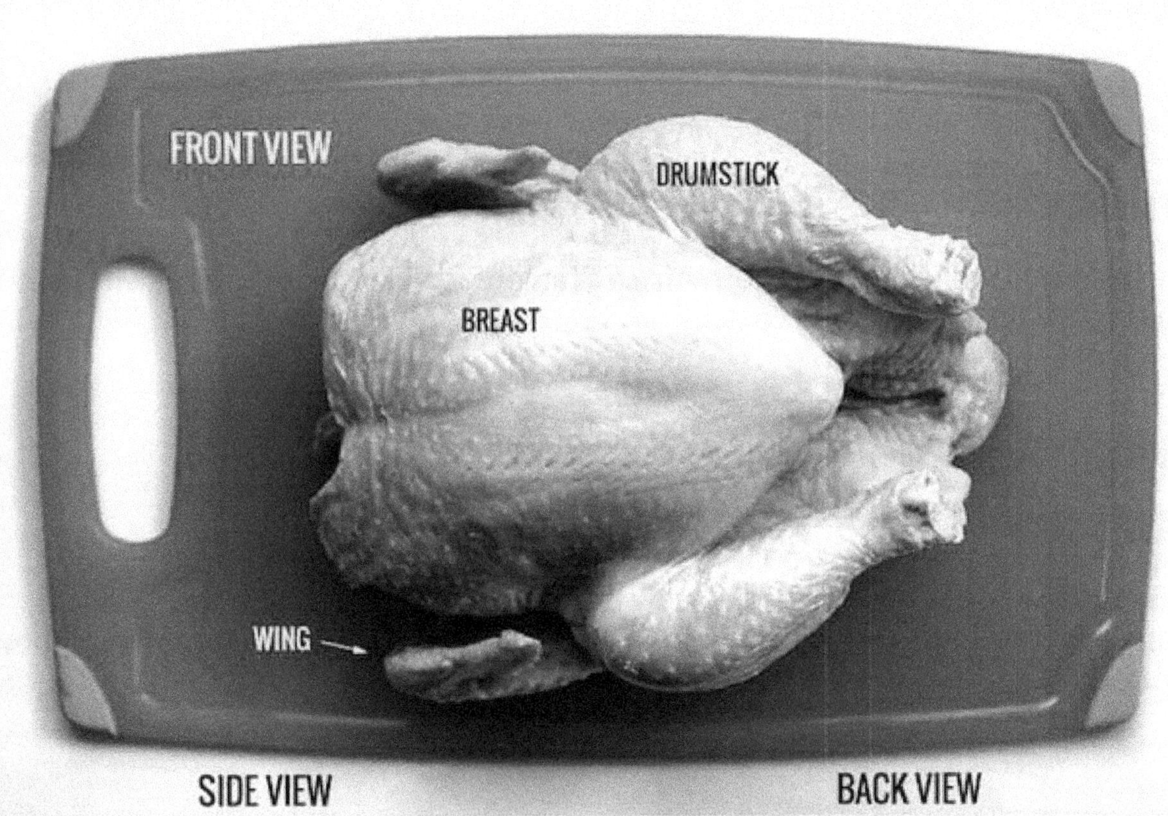

SIDE VIEW

BACK VIEW

ANATOMY OF THE CHICKEN

Head

The head is the talkie part of South Africa's famous walkie-talkies and stewing and braising are the best ways to cook it.

Breast

This very lean cut is best cooked quickly to keep them moist, for instance grilling, frying and braaiing. When stewing for braising breasts, don't overcook them as they will become dry and stringy.

Wing

Wings are high in fat and can withstand heat without becoming dry. They therefore are suited to deep- frying, braaiing and roasting. But however you cook them,

Tail

TAILS The tail is often attached to the thigh. It is packed with flavour because it contains a lot of fat and, thanks to the large skin area, becomes very crispy.

ANATOMY OF THE CHICKEN

Neck

This bony cut has very little meat but is an inexpensive way to flavour sauces and stock.

Thighs

Like drumsticks, thighs will be rather tough if not cooked properly. They have loads of fantastic flavour and are best when roasted or braised slowly or added to stews.

Drumstic

This popular cut could also be tough if it hasn't been cooked for long enough. The delicious dark brown meat particularly takes time and drumsticks taste best when they've been roasted, stewed, braised or braaied.

Feet

The other half of walkie-talkies, chicken feet are bony and low on meat. Once cooked, though, they are tender and can be eaten whole. Braai or grill them if you like crisp, crunchy skin.

HOW MANY CALORIES IN CHICKEN?

Chicken tenders

263 calories per 3.5 ounces (100 grams)

Back

137 calories per 3.5 ounces (100 grams)

Dark meat

125 calories per 3.5 ounces (100 grams)

Light meat

114 calories per 3.5 ounces (100 grams)

HOW MANY CALORIES IN CHICKEN?

Breast

A 3.5-ounce (100-gram) serving of chicken breast provides 165 calories, 31 grams of protein and 3.6 grams of fat.

Thigh

A 3.5-ounce (100-gram) serving of chicken thigh provides 209 calories, 26 grams of protein and 10.9 grams of fat.

Wing

Per 3.5 ounces (100 grams), chicken wings provide 203 calories, 30.5 grams of protein and 8.1 grams of fat.

Drumstick

Per 3.5 ounces (100 grams), chicken drumsticks have 172 calories, 28.3 grams of protein and 5.7 grams of fat.

Skin

While a skinless chicken breast is 284 calories with 80% protein and 20% fat, those numbers **dramatically** shift when you include the skin. One boneless, cooked chicken breast with skin (196 grams) contains: Calories: 386, Protein: 58.4 grams, Fat: 15.2 grams

COOKING METHODS

Grilling

This is one of the more common cooking methods, as it tends to require less added fat.

Baking or roasting

These other common methods are sufficient when you don't have access to a grill.

Broiling

This is similar to grilling, but you usually do it in a standard oven or toaster oven.

Braising

Lightly panfry the chicken and then cook it covered, submerged in liquid, for an extended time at a lower temperature.

COOKING METHODS

Fried

The chicken is submerged in hot cooking oil in either a pan or deep fryer. This creates a crisp outer coating but adds quite a bit of fat.

Baking or roasting

These other common methods are sufficient when you don't have access to a grill.

Boiling

You submerge the meat in boiling water and cook it until the internal temperature reaches 165°F (74°C). This is the leanest method, as it doesn't require added fats. Still, some may find the texture lacking.

Quick Recipes

Lemon Garlic Chicken

Place the whole roast chicken in the bakery with a whole lemon and a head of garlic (unpeeled) in the chicken cavity. Spice with salt and pepper. Cover with a lid and cook for 1-1 / 2 hours at 425 °. (Also try an orange).

Roasted Turkey Breast

Place the turkey breast in the bakery; Place 6-8 small red skinned potatoes, cut in half, around the turkey. Add 1/2 cup of white wine and 2 cloves of pressed garlic. Spice with salt and pepper. Cover with a lid. Bake at 350 ° F for 1-1 / 2 hours. Uncover for the last 15 to 20 minutes. Let stand 5 minutes before cutting.

Honey Mustard Chicken

Place the rotisserie chicken in the bakery and pour the fat-free honey mustard dressing on top. Cover with a lid. Roast 1-1 / 2 hours at 425 ° F.

3 CHEFS' TIPS
A little know-how can make life in the kitchen a lot easier

Done Yet

There are two ways to check if a chicken breast is done.
The first is to insert the tip of a small knife into the thickest part of the meat. If the juices run clear, it is cooked; if it's still pink,
you need to cook longer. Alternatively, make a small incision in the thickest part of the breast. If the meat is completely white and you don't see any pink meat, the brisket is done. The juices will also be clear. This method also works for testing whole chickens and other chicken pieces.

Slicing chicken breast for stir fry

Place the chicken breast, smooth side down, on a cutting board.
Cut diagonally into 1cm strips and cut each strip lengthwise in half into longer, thinner strips before cutting diagonally across the fibers to keep them tender.

Butterflying chicken breasts for schnitzels

Place the chicken breast smooth side down on a cutting board. Make a shallow incision along one side and continue as if you were trying to cut the breast into two identical halves. Stop just before cutting it all the way through, so the top and bottom half open like a book. With a meat mallet, tap the thickest part gently until it is finer and more uniform. Butterfly breasts can also be stuffed with any filling you like.

TIPS AND TRICKS

Keeping it Clean

- Once chicken has been defrosted, do not refreeze it.
- Don't let raw chicken come into contact with other food, cooked or uncooked.
- Always wash your hands, utensils and surfaces that have been in contact with raw chicken with hot, soapy water.
- Keep a separate chopping board for raw meat to prevent cross-contamination.
- Always make sure that meat is cooked through to kill all harmful bacteria that may have been lurking in it.

When buying chicken

Always look for chicken that has an even colour with no blemishes or bruises. The meat should look moist and plump and have a neutral smell. Check that the packaging hasn't been damaged in any way. When buying frozen chicken, make sure that the meat is frozen solid and does not have any soft areas where it has begun to defrost – and do remember to check the sell-by-date too.

Storing Chicken

Always refrigerate or freeze chicken as soon as possible after buying it. If the packet is damaged or soggy and you are going to cook it within two days, remove the chicken, pat it dry with kitchen paper and place on a plate. Cover with clingwrap or foil and put the plate on the bottom rack of the fridge. That way, it won't contaminate other food if it drips. If you want to freeze the chicken at home, remove it from the packet, pat it dry and reseal in an airtight bag.

TIPS AND TRICKS

Stop Breast Drying

How to stop the breast from drying out when MAKING roast chicken.
Roast the chicken breast-side down for two thirds of the cooking time. This way, all the juices will run down into the breast meat and keep it moist. Once you are ready to crisp the skin, carefully turn the chicken breast-side up and roast until golden.

How Tos and Hacks

Chicken salad. Place chicken breast side up on cutting board. Pull the
the leg and thigh away from the body and use your fingers to find the hip joint in the crease. Insert the tip of a large knife into the joint and cut through the skin, meat, and joint to separate the thigh and leg from the body. Repeat on the other side. Use
the same method to separate the leg from the thigh and cut the wings from the body.
To remove the chicken breast, cut the breast to divide the carcass in two. Cut all the bone and cartilage from the breasts.
You will now have two of each: thighs, drumsticks, wings, and breasts. Add the carcass to soups, stews or casseroles for flavor and remove the bones just before serving.

How to defrost a whole chicken

Thawing a frozen chicken is best done overnight in the fridge. Place it in a large bowl or on a plate to prevent the juices from dripping in the fridge. Before cooking it, check inside the cavity to see that there is no more ice. If pressed for time, put the bird in a bucket of cold water in the sink, but be sure to keep the water cold to prevent bacteria from growing.

TIPS AND TRICKS

Getting a golden skin

Check that the skin is completely dry, rub the whole bird generously with oil and season well.
Uncover the chicken 20-30 minutes before the end of the cooking time and place it on a shallow baking tray or on an oven rack on a tray to allow the dry heat to come into contact with as much skin as possible. Roast until the skin is crisp and glassy

Chicken and food poisoning

Raw chicken may contain natural bacteria, which could be dangerous if it hasn't been stored properly. Salmonella and campylobacter, which are linked to food poisoning and gastro, are among the most common.

3 DIPS FOR CHICKEN NUGGETS

Garlic and lemon mayo

Stir 2 finely chopped garlic cloves and zest and juice of 1/2 lemon into 1 cup (250 ml) Mayonnaise.

Tomato relish

Finely chop 3 small sherkins and 3 pickeled onions and stir into 3/4 cup (180ml) tomato sauce.

Sweet and sour

Stir together 3/4 cup (180 ml) pineapple juice, 1/4 cup (60 ml) apple cider vinegar, 1/4 cup (60 ml) brown sugar, 2 tbsp (30 ml) tomato cauce and 1 tbps (15 ml) cornflour. Thicker over a low heat.

Quick Recipes

Chicken Pot Pie

Simmer a couple of boneless, skinless chicken breasts, let cool and cube. Microwave cubed potatoes, carrots, celery, onion, green beans or peas. Combine with cornstarch-thickened chicken broth (from the simmered chicken), and pour into pie crust lined baker (you can use Pillsbury ready made) then top with the other crust, crimp, brush with milk, sprinkle with herbs, sesame seeds, or a little Parmesan, and bake at 350° about 40 min.

Cranberry Chicken

Mix one can of whole berry cranberries w/ can of cream of mushroom soup and one packet of onion soup mix. Pour over top of chicken in baker. Cover with lid, place in oven; bake for 1-1/2 hours at 425.

Chicken and Vegetables

Place chicken (skin on or off) in baker. Place chopped onion, celery and carrots around chicken. Sprinkle with 1/2 package of Good Seasons Italian Dressing mix. Place lid on top. Bake at 350° for 1 hour.

5 TIPS FOR GRILLED CHICKEN

Use bone in skin on chicken pieces

The thighs are highly recommended by grill experts, and I agree they are the most humid, but the legs, breasts, and wings also benefit when the bones and skin are left intact, as they help insulate the meat from overcooked and make it taste so much better.

(However, if you're committed to boneless, skinless chicken breasts, the techniques you practice with the remaining tips will help you master them with practice, too).

Pasture-raised chickens, especially those of traditional breeds, are not only tastier but also more sustainable than factory-farmed poultry, so look for them in your area at the farmer's market or local grocery store.

5 TIPS FOR GRILLED CHICKEN

Season chicken well with salt

Most people make their first mistake even before turning on the grill: they don't season the chicken enough.

Using your best quality kosher or sea salt, sprinkle all sides of the chicken pieces as if you were finely dusting them with powdered sugar.

Everyone loves marinated chicken, but dipping it into any sauce, even barbecue sauce, will bring you more cooking complications, not more flavor.

5 TIPS FOR GRILLED CHICKEN

Preheat your grill and flames under control

A diferencia de otros alimentos que responden bien al calor intenso, el pollo requiere un calor moderado o medio-alto (entre 350 F y 400 F).

Ya sea que use una parrilla de carbón o de gas, pruebe los patrones de calor colocando su palma abierta a unas 5 pulgadas por encima de la parrilla.

Si puede mantenerlo allí durante 5 segundos, está dentro del alcance.

También tenga en cuenta dónde el calor es menos intenso.

En caso de un brote, mueva inmediatamente el pollo a estas partes más frías de la parrilla para evitar que se queme.

5 TIPS FOR GRILLED CHICKEN

Brown chicken pieces skin side down

Always cook chicken skin side down first and plan to leave it there for the next 20 minutes or more, or until almost fully cooked.

Why? You'll end up with a crisp, beautifully browned skin (remember, isolate the meat), plus the chicken will cook evenly to the bone.

In general, it takes at least 30 minutes to cook bone-in chicken to this temperature, so try to cook it skin side down for three-quarters of the total cooking time (20 to 25 minutes) before turning. and finish it in the second. side.

5 TIPS FOR GRILLED CHICKEN

Use your grill as an oven

After placing the chicken pieces on the grill, cover.

Now your grill will radiate heat both up and down, which is exactly what your chicken needs to get fully cooked.

The lid also controls airflow and prevents the flames of a charcoal grill from getting out of control.

Fat dripping will likely cause breakouts, so monitor cooking and move chicken away from flames into cooler areas of the grill when necessary.

If you are not sure if the chicken is done, insert the tip of an instant read thermometer close to the bone or just cut in the center for a visual check.

The 5 Most Common Grilled Chicken Mistakes

Mistake n. 1
Not knowing the right cooking temperature for chicken

Mistake n. 2
Cooking too hot, lead to raw chicken too quickly

Mistake n. 3
Turn the chicken to the grill marks and get a blaze instead

Mistake n. 4
Finish with hard, dry chicken

Mistake n. 5
Grilled Chicken Sticks

The Great Chicken

USE SKIN-ON-BONE CHICKEN

The skin protects the meat from drying out and, along with the bone, adds a ton of flavor. Also, this method does not work with boneless, skinless chicken, which should be grilled quickly over high heat.

GET OUT OF THE COLD

Remove the chicken from the refrigerator and let it spread out at room temperature while the grill heats up. If the chicken is too cold when it hits the hot grill, the meat will tighten and become tough and may remain cold and raw near the bone even after the rest is well cooked.

MARINATE FOR EXTRA GOODNESS

You don't have to marinate, but if you do, you'll be rewarded with tastier meat. Marino at room temperature while the grill heats up. Enough time to season the meat (soaking chicken in sour marinades can make the consistency doughy). If you want to skip the marinade, sprinkle the chicken generously with kosher salt before letting it sit at room temperature.

MAKE SURE THE GRILL IS AT THE RIGHT TEMPERATURE

You want moderately high heat that registers 400 degrees on a built-in thermometer when the lid is closed. Turn the knobs on a gas grill between the highest and medium setting. On a charcoal grill, distribute the incinerated coals in an even layer. The coals are ready when you can hold your hand a thumb above the grill for 3 seconds before instinctively walking away.

PREPARE THE CHICKEN SKIN

Just before placing the chicken on the grill, wipe off the excess marinade, then pull the chicken skin over the meat to cover it as much as possible. If there is extra skin on the thighs (lucky!), Wrap it over the skinless parts. This will help the skin brown evenly and keep the meat more tender. Place the chicken on the hot grill with the skin side down.

DO NOT MOVE THE MEAT

Cover the grill, opening the top vents on a charcoal grill. In this first stage of cooking, you want the skin to turn a deep golden brown. When ready, it will naturally break free from the grill. If it starts to brown too quickly, lower the heat. If you try to flip it over and it clings to the grill, let it sit longer.

TASTE THE MEAT

After flipping the chicken, cook it skin side up until the meat is almost cooked if you are going to glaze it and if not, it is fully cooked. To test the doneness, slide a sharp kitchen knife close to the bone. It should slide in and out easily and the blade should be hot. Any juices that run out should be clear. If you have an accurate meat thermometer, meat close to the bone should register 160 degrees for bone-in breasts and 165 degrees for dark meat.

GLASS EVENLY AND FINISH

COOKING

If you are glazing the chicken with the sauce, brush the skin with a generous layer when the meat is almost cooked (155 degrees for the brisket; 160 for the legs). Turn it over and brush the other side. Continue glazing and brushing at a steady pace until the chicken has a coat of caramelized sauce.

WAIT FOR IT

When you take the chicken off the grill, you'll be drooling from its smoky scent. But resist the temptation to do it right away. Let the chicken rest on the uncovered tray for about five minutes before serving. This will make the meat juicier and let the glaze soak up its flavor.

USE SKIN-ON-BONE CHICKEN

The skin protects the meat from drying out and, along with the bone, adds a ton of flavor. Also, this method does not work with boneless, skinless chicken, which should be grilled quickly over high heat.

GET OUT OF THE COLD

Remove the chicken from the refrigerator and let it spread out at room temperature while the grill heats up. If the chicken is too cold when it hits the hot grill, the meat will tighten and become tough and may remain cold and raw near the bone even after the rest is well cooked.

MARINATE FOR EXTRA GOODNESS

You don't have to marinate, but if you do, you'll be rewarded with tastier meat. Marino at room temperature while the grill heats up. Enough time to season the meat (soaking chicken in sour marinades can make the consistency doughy). If you want to skip the marinade, sprinkle the chicken generously with kosher salt before letting it sit at room temperature.

MAKE SURE THE GRILL IS AT THE RIGHT TEMPERATURE

You want moderately high heat that registers 400 degrees on a built-in thermometer when the lid is closed. Turn the knobs on a gas grill between the highest and medium setting. On a charcoal grill, distribute the incinerated coals in an even layer. The coals are ready when you can hold your hand a thumb above the grill for 3 seconds before instinctively walking away.

PREPARE THE CHICKEN SKIN

Just before placing the chicken on the grill, wipe off the excess marinade, then pull the chicken skin over the meat to cover it as much as possible. If there is extra skin on the thighs (lucky!), Wrap it over the skinless parts. This will help the skin brown evenly and keep the meat more tender. Place the chicken on the hot grill with the skin side down.

DO NOT MOVE THE MEA

Cover the grill, opening the top vents on a charcoal grill. In this first stage of cooking, you want the skin to turn a deep golden brown. When ready, it will naturally break free from the grill. If it starts to brown too quickly, lower the heat. If you try to flip it over and it clings to the grill, let it sit longer.

TASTE THE MEAT

After flipping the chicken, cook it skin side up until the meat is almost cooked if you are going to glaze it and if not, it is fully cooked. To test the doneness, slide a sharp kitchen knife close to the bone. It should slide in and out easily and the blade should be hot. Any juices that run out should be clear. If you have an accurate meat thermometer, meat close to the bone should register 160 degrees for bone-in breasts and 165 degrees for dark meat.

GLASS EVENLY AND FINISH COOKING

If you are glazing the chicken with the sauce, brush the skin with a generous layer when the meat is almost cooked (155 degrees for the brisket; 160 for the legs). Turn it over and brush the other side. Continue glazing and brushing at a steady pace until the chicken has a coat of caramelized sauce.

Lightning Source UK Ltd.
Milton Keynes UK
UKHW051435100621
385263UK00002B/352